CHRISTOPHER NYE

MAXIMUMDINER

Making it Big in Uckfield

Acknowledgments

Neither the Maximum Diner nor this book would ever have happened without the ceaseless nagging of my brother Jeremy; extra special thanks also to Simon, Louise and my mother for all their love, support and cash. Thank you to all the wonderful staff and customers in Uckfield, especially to Liz, Catherine, Laura, Sally, Malcolm, Nigel, Claudia, Zita, Imogen, Cathy, Emma, and Sarah at the Riverside (for all the teacakes). And an enormous thankyou to Nat Jansz and Mark Ellingham for sensitively bashing my manuscript into shape.

Sort Of Books thank Peter Dyer, Henry Iles, Nikky Twyman, Rachel Partridge, Lance Chinnian, Sarah Barber, Andrew Stephenson and Isabel Hudson.

The events described in this book took place, but – to protect Uckfield's fine upstanding folk – the names of various characters have been changed, along with their attributes. If anyone recognises themselves in these pages, the author hopes it will be with pleasure. The Maximum Diner, after all, was a lot of fun.

Maximum Diner. Copyright © 2004 by Christopher Nye.
No part of this book may be reproduced in any form without permission from the publisher except for the quotation of brief passages in reviews.

Published in 2004 by Sort Of Books, PO Box 18678, London NW3 2FL.
Distributed by the Penguin Group in all territories excluding the United States and Canada: Penguin Books, 80 Strand, London WC2R 0RL.
Typeset in Minion to a design by Henry Iles.
Printed in Suffolk by Clays.
224pp.
A catalogue record for this book is available from the British Library.
ISBN 0-9542217-3-7

Contents

Premises, Premises

UCKFIELD IS A BUSY LITTLE TOWN of around 15,000 people, set in the East Sussex Weald. For those not familiar with the area, this is a rather soggy strip of land south of London, between two ranges of hills called the North and South Downs (I have no idea why hills are called Downs). There's a High Weald and Low Weald, but let's not get too technical; the point is, if you were driving from London to Brighton and just before reaching the South Downs decided to turn left towards nowhere in particular, you might well end up in Uckfield.

This small country town has relatively few claims to fame. Its High Street used to get blocked with traffic heading for Eastbourne but they fixed that with a bypass. Lord Lucan was last sighted here. There was a train crash once, but despite five people dying it was barely reported; and the river that dribbles through the town centre – the Uck – floods occasionally. And that's about it. Uckfield could easily be dismissed as a little dull.

Yet I've always liked the place. The shops, which are crammed into the High Street that leads up from the dribbly river, may not be particularly exciting but they are useful – which kind of sums up the town. If you want to buy a plastic washing-up bowl for a pound, or try a new brand of economy toilet tissue, you're spoilt for choice in Uckfield. Unlike in Lewes, eight miles down the road, you would be pressed to find a 1930s Bakelite flyswat or organic underwear (really, you can buy pants made of fair-traded, organic cotton in Lewes), but no one seems to mind.

The countryside around isn't much to write home about, either, at least not since East Sussex's planners discovered the wheeze of circling villages in the Low Weald with new bypasses, so as to preserve the ambience of the traditional high streets, and then developing all the land in between. Acres of brand new semi-detached houses, each with faux-Victorian porches, little arched windows and calf-high conifer trees, now greet the happy motorist off for a meander round the country lanes.

Pretty countryside, however, wasn't much of an issue for me. Uckfield's pull was that it was in Sussex – I lived in Brighton at the time and preferred to stick to home turf – and that it met the exacting demographic conditions laid out in my business plan. I had figured that there had to be a demand in small towns for the kind of cheap, convenient, fast food service that McDonald's and the other burger chains were providing in the big ones. All I had to do was find a big enough small town – say 10,000 to 20,000 people – that was far enough away from the competition, then launch my own brand new business. The other details, like where the money would come from, were a little hazy. But Uckfield looked a promising place to start.

I knew this not from an idle whim but from sound scientific principles. I'd bought a map of Sussex, some coloured flags and the most recent census figures from the library, and had stuck flags into centres of the right size and with a number of satellite

2

villages around but no large town or city within half an hour's drive. Another flag showed roughly how many properties were for sale. Burgess Hill, for instance, had no empty shops; Newhaven had too many; Uckfield, yet again, showed a full hand.

This may be a male thing, but there's nothing quite like putting a giant map on the wall and sticking coloured flags in it to make you feel you're getting along in the world. In hindsight it all seems so momentous, or *meant*. When I stuck a red flag on Uckfield, I imagined myself Christopher Plummer playing the Duke of Wellington, casting a languid yet intelligent eye at the map before tapping it and saying, 'Let us rest for the night here... at Waterloo.' Around him groups of young officers would shrug or nod, little realising that at this very spot most of them were going to wind up dead.

In reality my flag-sticking was more like Alan Titchmarsh pointing to a chart and saying, 'Let us put the lupins in here, by the bush.' However, at least I was acting scientifically and in so doing was giving my business a fighting chance of succeeding where so many others would fail. The census figures showed that Uckfield had a good population density per household, such a huge percentage of children that it was officially the youngest town in Sussex, reasonable earnings, low unemployment, high levels of car ownership, and several other statistics that I wasn't sure as to the significance of but factored in as positives anyway (like dog distribution, average number of foreign holidays per year, percentage of people with separate sofa insurance). The picture formed was of an aspirational town, for people who've chosen their partner, are well on the way to 2.4 kids, and are settled into their career and the housing ladder. And hundreds more seemed to be joining them each year.

3

Kind friends warned me not to waste my efforts in the sticks, but to aim straight for the big time. Like Brighton. But Brighton's not really that big time, is it? London is big time and so is New York, and maybe Paris – but Brighton? Anyway, the place was already crammed with grungy student cafés, ex-Londoners opening designer bistros, and extended family businesses with the entrepreneurial spirit and stamina to stay open until 3am. So why follow the herd?

Besides which, as I patiently explained, I *like* small towns. Not enough to spend my life in one, perhaps, but from a philosophical angle they strike me as an entirely good thing: dependable, unpretentious, manageable. I didn't want to open just another miserably insignificant little business in the city; my place was going to be the talk of the town, and then another town, and another...

Also, leases and rents are cheap in small towns, and since I didn't have any serious amount of money the option of opening big in Brighton or anywhere else was pretty much closed.

I took myself off to Uckfield for the day. With the morning sun winking back at me from rows of faux-leaded window panes, I drove past the outlying housing estates and into the centre of town. I was humming a medley from *The Sound of Music* as I always do on bright, optimistic, start-of-a-new-life mornings, and mulling over the outrageous good fortune that had begun the day. Amanda had phoned. What could possibly augur better than that?

4   Amanda was a beautiful, stylish (some might say out-of-my-league) colleague from the Hotel Metropole, who for a blissful week and a half had promoted me from a shoulder to cry on to temporary lover. I didn't care that it was on the rebound – her wine importer boyfriend having just ditched her for a teenager from Bordeaux. I just hoped I could turn myself into a habit. Sadly, the dream shattered when I lost my job. Amanda had an absolute rule against unemployed boyfriends and, eerily

mirroring the terminology of management, informed me she would have to 'let me go'. (She had a weakness for jargon that I used to find endearing.) But that was then. Amanda had obviously undergone some Road to Damascus enlightenment; she hadn't even asked me to diarise the date. Now all I needed was a career plan to impress her with, maybe a mission statement or two. Becoming Uckfield's very own Mr Budgen, or the Rocco Forte of the Road to Eastbourne, was surely a good place to start.

I parked my battered Ford Escort van next to a sign reading 'River Uck', clearly a site of relentless struggle between the council and the town's graffiti artists. In an effort to snatch victory the council had painted the two words one on top of the other with the 'U' hard up against the edge of the board, leaving no space at all to insinuate even the scrawniest letter. Paradoxically, this created the impression that an 'F' had been sawn off, and consequently seemed to hang beside it like an after-image. Or perhaps it was an 'M'.

The Uck flowed in a thin, mucky line along a V-shaped canyon heading for the equally unromantic Upper Ouse and the sea. A Tesco trolley, some traffic cones and an overturned wheelie bin had been dumped into the canyon, detracting slightly from its riverbank qualities. But I was in no mood anyway to linger by this interesting arterial waterway; I had a task at hand. I had to find myself some premises, and survey the competition.

Walking up Uckfield High Street, the first potential competitor I discovered was a Starburger, which is a bit like a Wimpy only less classy. The surfaces were covered with bright-red and white tiles whose grimy grouting and scuffed Formica put me in mind of a 1970s East German crèche. The waiter seemed friendly enough, though, and waved me towards a table, offering to bring a cappuccino. I was a bit surprised they had such a sophisticated range of drinks, to be honest, and I was surprised again when the coffee arrived, to find instead of the traditional sprinkle of

5

chocolate, the froth was liberally covered with instant coffee granules. Still, I like a bit of innovation, so I gave the waiter a cheery, encouraging thumbs up and stirred it in.

I walked further up the High Street popping into all the other competitors. There was a cakeshop-cum-café called The Three Cooks that had five bad-tempered ladies shifting savoury pastries around a heated cabinet and shooing kids away from the metal sides. There was Brandons, a teashop staffed by teenage girls smiling bravely through the embarrassment of wearing frilly lime-green tabards. and then, nearing the end of the row, The Charcoal Grill, one of those old-fashioned kebab shops that attempt to entice passing customers by rotating a sweaty, bone-less lump of meaty substance in the window (how do the Environmental Health people allow that?). It also had a boarded-up door panel. I later discovered that the owner had been flung through it during some festive high jinks at the recent Uckfield Carnival. Kids, eh?

Further and further up the hill I climbed, munching on a sausage roll from The Five Stroppy Women and enjoying the sights of small town life. At the hardware and kitchen shop beside the crossroads, two large stars had been cut out from Day-Glo cardboard and stuck to the window advertising the shop's special attractions: 'TOYS,' shouted one; 'TOILETRIES,' screamed the other. Although impressed with their clever use of alliteration and broad family appeal, I couldn't help but feel there might be room in Uckfield for some new marketing ideas – ones I would be happy to demonstrate if I could only find premises from which to do so.

The road became steeper, but I ploughed on, undaunted by the stiff climb and blazing heat. No, indeed; I was ready to climb every mountain and ford every stream. This was my first mistake. If you have to make an extra effort to find a place, then so too will your customers. The phrase 'Location, location, location' was first used by Lord Forte to explain the three key factors in the success of any catering enterprise (I don't know where 'serving edible food' was ranked). Before opening his first milk bar in the 1930s, the young Forte stood outside the earmarked site, counting, as he put it, 'all of the mouths walking past'.

These days choosing the right location is a little more complex, because people have so much more choice, so much less time, and cars. A pedestrianised high street location is great for Saturday lunchtimes but might become a barren hooliganised no-go area in the evenings. Parking, or a nearby off-licence, cinema or video shop can be crucial. But, in essence, location should be a no-brainer. Once you've established, through meticulous analysis, a location for your new business, the decision about the actual site comes down to one simple question: 'Will anyone actually go there?' After that you need to ask: 'Yes, but will they really?' And then perhaps: 'No but really, I mean will they?' and: 'Hmm, really?' You just can't be too sceptical.

Further up the High Street I reached a little crossroads and some traffic lights, and was rewarded with the road levelling out into a little plateau. Gasping for breath and with a stitch in my side, I found myself in a 'secondary trading area' of quiet little shops and takeaways. This was the old town, set on a relatively flat bit halfway up the valley side, above the floodplain and on the medieval pilgrim road between Chichester and Canterbury. Centuries ago, weary pilgrims would rest here for the night, clean the mud from their robes and look around for a nice leg of mutton and some mead to wash it down with. Nowadays they'd have to find what pickings they could from an anglers' supplier, wedding hire shop, two barbers, an opticians, an off-licence and a Chinese takeaway.

A lovely little collection of shops, and useful, too. But not many people were shopping in them, and had I been counting 'the mouths walking past' I could have done it on the fingers of one

7

hand. There was, nonetheless, a clear sense of community, easy parking and a property with a 'For Sale' sign over it that seemed to have been placed there by destiny's hand. It was a small, sophisticated little bistro called Cain's.

I gazed in through the window. Cain's really was small – just six tables and a counter – but there was something about it that snagged on the heartstrings. It was compact, but light and airy. And it had a drinks licence. This was the site that I'd been dreaming about.

Twenty minutes later I was pacing back up the hill from the estate agent's office with the bistro's owner. Kevin was a large bloke – a bit too large I would have thought to work in a tiny little bistro – but he had the sort of calm, relaxed manner that fits in anywhere. He was about my age, though way ahead in matters of local business. As well as Cain's, he owned the local cinema, which he had turned in less than a year from a standard small town cinema (the same films as everyone else, a month or two late) into one of the best independent movie houses in the country. Not only did he know everything about the catering trade but the man was a walking *Halliwell's*. Also, presumably in the odd moment between threading celluloid reels and whizzing round with the cheese board, he had co-written a comedy TV sketch show called *Six Pairs of Pants*. No, I hadn't heard of it either, but it all contributed to a very favourable impression of a cheery, can-do, talented sort of man.

So why exactly did I jump to the conclusion that I could do better than Kevin and make a go of the restaurant where he had struggled to scrape a profit? What did I have that the polymath of Uckfield could have lacked? The answer was simple. I had a vision. I wasn't going to run a bistro – no, obviously bistros were a big mistake – I was going to buy the site with its drinks licence and permission for A3 use (allowing the cooking and selling and eating of food on the premises) and turn it into an American-style diner. Anyone with any sense at all would realise that a diner was the natural choice for the site. Diners were small – they had to be, since they were designed to be loaded, fully prefabricated, onto railroad carriages and transported right across America. They were the perfect vehicle for the fast food domination of small town Britain.

Kevin was fascinated. He'd wondered about opening a diner himself, he admitted, popping the top off a beer and sliding it across the counter, ever since he'd seen the Barry Levinson movie, *Diner*. Had I seen it, he asked? I almost choked on my Becks. Had Tony Soprano seen *The Godfather*? Had the Pope ever seen *Song of Bernadette*? *Diner* was one of my all-time seminal influences. It was the film that, in my late teens, launched me across the States doing Jack Kerouac impersonations, hitching rides and washing up and waiting at table. Diners were my sort of places – hip, friendly and with none of the class war hang-ups, or crappy food, of the greasy spoons. They were the people's cafés, unapologetic and appetising. Also it just so happens that I lost my virginity with a waitress who worked in a diner near Pennsylvania. (She admired my English accent, slipped me a free apple pie, and asked if I'd like it *à la mode*. Well, I didn't need asking twice.) And suddenly here I was within a hair's breadth of owning and running such an establishment myself.

I didn't, of course, confide all this to Kevin. Only a sucker shows that amount of enthusiasm while trying to buy a lease. But we did knock the idea around in a not-uninterested kind of way. Kevin even knew some decent organic butchers who might be happy to do a deal on mince, though he wasn't sure the margins would work out. And, of course, he could throw in a load of equipment and sort me out with a good joiner for the

9

fittings. I nodded in a sort of insouciant 'don't mind if I do, don't mind if I don't' sort of way and asked about the evening crowd. It was alright, Kevin asserted, buoyant if not exactly heaving. He suggested I came back that night for a meal 'on the house' and check it out. I said I was busy but would try and drop round in a couple of days' time.

That was a lie. Later that same night I cut the lights on the van and manoeuvred stealthily into position to watch the comings and goings at Cain's. I was equipped with a pad, pens and a secret torch.

Covert surveillance isn't as easy as you might suppose. It's mind-numbingly boring, for one. And then it's all too easy to find yourself getting paranoid as you start believing that everyone else is spying on you, rather than you on them. I had parked outside the off-licence and became convinced that the lady in the shop was ringing the police in the expectation of me robbing her. Worse than this, my stomach was rumbling. In any decent film the stake-out is conducted with a plastic beaker of coffee in one hand and a hot pastrami and rye in the other, giving a light, if slightly greasy, touch to the gathering suspense. I, however, had turned down a very decent free dinner, a rare steak and sorbet perhaps, with maybe a wine from the Medoc, consumed in the friendly glow of Cain's, to sit in the dark sucking on a boiled travel sweet. It didn't seem such a great swap.

Then a whole load of youths sat on my bonnet and began shouting at passers-by to get them some cans from the off-licence. I didn't want to hoot at them and risk blowing my cover, but I felt unmanly letting them just sit there and, besides, they were blocking my view of Cain's. A few of them were passing round a joint, which seemed to help them, in a contemplative sort of way, to come up with new and creative reasons for abusing passing strangers. So, convincing myself that twenty minutes' spying is more than enough to get a good impression of a place, I started the engine and, much to their surprise, drove off.

The area had certainly seemed to have its share of Uckfield's night-time action. Not quite the same slice as Piccadilly Circus or even the kiosk by the bus station, but it had a decent number of 'mouths' for a secondary shopping area up a steep hill. My mind was almost made up.

I mentioned that I had already made my first mistake. But I was making a second, equally momentous one, in choosing somewhere so small. The point of fast food isn't so much that it's fast, but that it's convenient. Its customers will always take the easiest option: not the best, or even the best value, just the easiest. They don't want to walk anywhere, least of all up a hill, when there's a chance that all six tables will be full, not if there's an empty table waiting for them much closer to home.

Take me, for instance. There's an Indian takeaway not far from my flat that has convictions (note, actual convictions!) for putting too much colouring in the curry sauces. But I can park outside the place and I have their number programmed into my mobile phone, so... forgive and forget. At least, until their competitors get parking spaces.

A little ironically, I was setting myself up by the very same rules of the game. I was being seduced by convenience, unwilling to stop and think earnestly about the shortcomings of the site. The search for suitable premises can take years but catering people are not the most patient types. Most chefs have to plan, prepare, execute, clear up and get paid for their work over the course of a lunchtime. We just don't have the mentality to grow a project

11

quietly to fruition. That's more for your cathedral architect, or Giant Sequoia plantation manager.

And there were other pressing reasons for plumping for Cain's. I was due to meet Amanda for dinner the next evening and felt I could do a much better impersonation of the dashing young businessman if I actually had a business under offer. Cain's was available, which was a good thing, and it had planning permission and a drinks licence, which was manna from heaven.

So Cain's it had to be.

There was just one small fly in the ointment. Kevin was asking £18,000 for the business. It was quite a concession, he said, as he'd paid almost double himself, three years earlier, and he led me to believe there could be room for negotiation. But this was still a little more than I could slap on the table – well, £18,000 more, to tell the truth. I made thoughtful, appreciative noises down the phone to Kevin and told him I was keen and would get back to him about it. Then I phoned my local high-street bank and booked an appointment.

What Ray Kroc
would have said

IF I'D ASKED THE ADVICE OF THE MCDONALD BROTHERS or their friend and mentor, Ray Kroc, I would have been told to forget the diner idea, it would never work. Even in their heyday, in 1950s America, diners didn't stand a chance against the new branded burger franchises that were springing up around them. The good folks of southern California, home to the first McDonald's, might have thought they cared about the tiny, downhome Mom-and-Pop-style diners with their personal service, neighbourliness and good food cooked to order, but actually they didn't give a stuff about any of that.

Ray Kroc realised, with the insight of a true innovator, that all his customers cared about was having tasty, cheap food, served to them cleanly, consistently and, above all, quickly. Nor did it matter if there was hardly any choice, so long as the item ordered (burgers and fried potatoes in their case) was exactly the same as the last time they ordered it. For this new generation of American baby-boomers, getting food would be a simple biological imperative, not an expressive act that defined them as human beings in any way. So restaurant food, like other convenience foods (tinned, frozen, whatever), could be prepared in an assembly line system and served without any meaningful human interaction whatsoever.

In fact, Ray Kroc decided that it was an inconvenience for staff even to have emotions: happy one day, unhappy the next – an attitude like that could affect customers and influence sales. So he decided that all the servers would say, to every customer, 'Have a nice day!' It was simple, short and right to the point. Enjoy your day. Don't have a bad day. I really hope nothing terrible happens to you today, but don't go overboard with something spectacular – just nice, okay? Well, who but the most curmudgeonly wouldn't like to have their day blessed? Furthermore, there seemed no more need to motivate their staff or make any attempt to keep them happy in their work – even if said sarcastically, in the hubbub of a busy takeaway, the customer was hardly going to notice.

Of course some were bound to wring their hands and lament: Where's the humanity? Where's the generosity, the spirit, the human warmth? To which Ray Kroc might have retorted: But did we ever really care about all that? Didn't the upper classes value their servants specifically for their ability to keep their mouths shut, and not spill the consommé? If you open a tin of beans, does it matter whether or not you've had a nice chat with the person who put it in the tin? It's just food; convenience food, brought to the customer with the minimum of fuss, bother or expense. Sure, some people still think they want chatty, informal little cafés with personality, just as some people have a nostalgia for the sweet shop on the corner or the local greengrocer's, but they're just kidding themselves. Really they only want some-where to drive to and be fed.

Well, that's what the founders of the world's most successful fast food chain, with no fewer than 28,000 restaurants world-wide, might have said. But it cut no ice with me. What did they know about Uckfield?

And in any case, these points were irrelevant because there was no competition for my diner. The nearest McDonald's, as I had already ascertained, was fifteen miles away in Brighton and no application for planning permission had been lodged by any of the fast food chains. Uckfield was a frontier town in catering terms, ready and waiting to be re-educated about the joys of eating at a small, local, stylish diner that served good food with all the efficiency of the big brand outlets. And I was the man who was going to show them how to do it.

I was talking a big game and Amanda, when we met in our old hotel bar, was impressed. In fact she was more than impressed. There was something about the words 'franchise' and 'brand expansion' that seemed to genuinely excite her, although admit-tedly the effect was slightly weakened by other words like 'Uckfield' and 'burgers'. For a moment the air crackled with sexual chemistry, and I was gripped by that light-headed feeling you get when you know you're just one tiny gesture away from beginning foreplay. And then her mobile phone rang. For the next half hour she gave a soft, breathy, intimate summary of all my business hopes and assets to someone called Guy, before happily inviting him to drive over and join us.

While we waited, Amanda explained that Guy was a friend of the family and an incredibly talented venture capitalist. She just knew that he would be the right person to fund the project. 'He's

15

so shrewd and experienced,' she enthused. 'And I just know you two are really going to like each other.' Somehow I doubted it.

My intuition was spot-on.

'Why don't you offer this Kevin character nothing at all for his place?' was Guy's opening suggestion, as he leant back in his seat and flicked the keyring of his new Lexus against his palm.

'What do you mean by "nothing"?' I asked, appalled.

'Yes, what do you mean?' asked Amanda, her eyes brightening at the thought.

What he meant was exactly that – a zero offer. Kevin was stuck with a lease but was probably sick to death of spending every evening cooking and serving food in a restaurant he had already mentally sold, knowing that every minute he devoted to it put his more lucrative enterprise, the cinema, in jeopardy. I should take advantage of his weak bargaining position, Guy argued, and show a to-hell-with-it buccaneering spirit.

He had a point, of course. Amanda was nodding emphatically. Paying nothing made a lot of sense to her too, and if I could swing it, well, it would be a smart investment, wouldn't it?

'Sure,' agreed Guy with a sneery grin. 'Come and see me, Christopher, when you've got your answer, and we'll hang a few ideas from the flagpole and see who salutes.'

Even without his muscling in on my ex-lover and demoting me to gooseberry of the group, I knew that Guy and I were never going to get on. Desperation, however, breeds strange alliances and I really did need his cash. So, to my utter shame, I wrote to Kevin and offered to take Cain's off his hands for free.

I didn't hear back. But that was okay, I reassured myself, because I could play it cool too. More days passed. I called Amanda to see if she fancied a night out, while I continued to play it cool, but she couldn't spare an evening. I phoned Guy to see if he had any more tactics up his sleeve, like maybe bringing money into the equation. But no, he insisted – it was bound to be bumpy at first, Kevin just needed a little bit longer to face up to realities.

Meanwhile, my appointment with the bank arrived.

At polytechnic, studying for our degrees, we budding hospitality executives spent many hours looking at sources of finance. I must have passed exams on it, but all I remember now about the theory was that there's something called 'gearing'. Education, eh? What it boils down to are four simple options: either you spend your own money, your family's, someone else's (Guy's, ideally), or the bank's.

Self was out of the question for the usual, very simple, fiscal reasons. Family was a possibility. My older brother, Simon, had recently made a packet writing a TV script and was one of those effortlessly generous types who think of good fortune as a privilege that ought to be shared – a mad idea that could start revolutions if it caught on. But what if the diner failed? Could I face him every year, across the Christmas turkey, while his children played with their plastic treats from Toys'n'Toiletries? Or, worse, would I project my own shame back onto him in some complex 'why did you let me ruin both our lives' sort of way? 17

Guy would be an easier option. Guy was one of those venture capitalists who want to invest in a more entertaining way than just putting their stock market earnings back into the stock market. But in return for the risk he'd expect a higher rate of interest. That would mean his taking a large part of my profit, as well as getting to interfere endlessly and swanning in whenever for free meals. On the plus side, people like Guy are a lot more business-orientated and experienced than your average bank manager and can give you quite useful advice. Also, unlike with family, should you go bust you can walk away from the wreckage whistling cheerfully.

Banks, of course, are the pits. They care only about making profit; they are not your friend or 'business angel' (they have no more idea about cutting-edge business than the paperboy) and they will do you no favours. Frankly, they don't even like you, which is why half their branches have turned into wine bars. However, come up with some cash yourself, something to show your own commitment, and they may lend you a bit more or give you an overdraft. Then, as soon as they possibly can, they'll be charging you £29.50 each time they bounce a direct debit.

I reflected on this as I sat outside the manager's office clutching a smart plastic folder with all my research into food and equipment costs, some terrific photos of American diners, floor plans, graphs of projected revenues and profits, and so on. I still have the file – it's beautiful. And it wasn't all bollocks, either: over years of working in hotels and restaurants I'd learnt that it's the drip of unforeseen and unbudgeted-for expenses (National Insurance, van repairs, rodent control) that can bring a business down, and I'd even factored a few of these into the plan.

The bank manager ushered me in. He was a tall, affable chap, who smiled patiently at me as he explained the basic banking tenets of risk and reward using the objects on his desk.

18   'Imagine this is the bank's money,' he urged, indicating the stapler. 'And I lend some of it to you.' He pushed the stapler tentatively across the desk to me. 'Eventually, we're going to want it back,' and he pulled the stapler back towards him with both hands, 'with what we call interest. In-ter-est. But, do you know' – a note of solemnity crept into his voice – 'often we don't get it back because most new catering businesses fail before they've even got to the end of their first year?'

He moved the stapler to the side of the desk furthest away from both of us, where it sat isolated from the biro and hole puncher. The bank manager and I both stared at it glumly for a moment.

'Now, about your overdraft...'

During the lecture he had slyly pushed my diner file further and further away from him across the desk, and now he began rifling through his own files looking for the account numbers of chequebooks and cards he intended to confiscate before yet another direct debit presented itself. Seven minutes later I was back on the street, stripped of any immediate means of getting cash, and hugging my diner folder protectively, as if it was a child who had just come last in a Beautiful Baby competition.

Oh well, I didn't need a loan just yet anyway. I still hadn't heard from Kevin and I had found no other even vaguely suitable property. I took some shift work, cash in hand, at the first hotel with room service vacancies and began to look around again in earnest.

Catering is such a hard, grimy, competitive living, you would expect to see plenty of failing businesses appear on the market each month. But you don't. In reality very few get advertised and only a small number of these come with vacant possession, presumably because their owners, having coughed up the huge opening costs, prefer to hang on grimly in the hopes of recouping their investment. The prices they ask, therefore, can be outrageously high.

Initially it's hard to imagine how their owners have the nerve to ask £30,000-plus for, say, a greasy spoon on a lonely windswept ring road, or a burger van in the car park of a B&Q; but they do. And all too often people pay these prices, perpetuating the cycle of unsustainable debt.

The difference between buying a business and buying a private house is that with a house one tends to be trying to buy into the lifestyle of the present owner – you're not necessarily expecting to exceed their lifestyle. But with a business, you look rather contemptuously at the current owner, noting with all your business acumen and vision what they've done wrong. You see only potential and what riches that business can bring if you get it right (which obviously you will).

So £30,000, you might reason, if you're in a property for ten years, is only three grand a year, less than £60 a week. Not much at all, when the overall costs of running that business might run into thousands of pounds each week. Not much, either, as an alternative to waiting four to twelve months for cheaper premises, or planning permission, or to build your own space from scratch. Heck! You could have earned twice £30,000 in that time!

There are pluses and minuses to that kind of thinking. On the minus side, as Mr Stapler had observed, well over fifty percent of catering businesses fail before the end of their first year, often for reasons beyond the control of the existing owners. It might be something indefinably wrong with the site. On some sites, shop after shop, restaurant after restaurant, have opened to a fanfare only to be picked over by bailiffs a few months later. Some London friends once asked me to help open an Australian steakhouse in an empty shop in Brighton. There was plenty of 'footfall' and 'mouths going past' but over the previous twelve years I'd seen the premises open and close as a bikers' pub, a Ratpack-themed cocktail bar, an Egyptian carpet emporium and a bedding shop (The Bedding Shop: 'We Don't Just Sell Bedding'), and most often stand empty save for the fading signs of the previous occupants. Maybe there was some invisible force stopping customers from going in, something in the look of the place that wasn't quite right. Maybe it was built on an ancient

Bronze Age burial mound. Maybe there was an over-rapacious landlord. Whatever the reason, I advised my friends, it just wouldn't work. (Funnily enough, there's now a massively successful restaurant there and my friends are quite cross about my advice but, hey, who could have predicted that?)

I let another fortnight pass and then I contacted Kevin. He was understandably a little cool, bristly even, but it's amazing what a frank and full apology, with a bit of grovelling thrown in, can do. I explained about Guy – we agreed he was a complete tosser – and about my hopes of linking up with him for the money. He offered the advice that I should try family first, and then, to show no hard feelings, dropped the price to £15,000. I was thrilled.

Guy was outraged. It was completely mad, he insisted. How would I have any capital to properly kit out the place? How could I afford uniforms for valet parking if Kevin demanded so much for the lease? The question took me by surprise. What valet parking? What uniform? For some reason, employing someone wearing Michael Jackson cast-offs to park your customers' cars while they enjoyed a carefree meal was the pivot of Guy's business idea. I listened politely, and told him I'd be happy to park his car for him whenever he or any friends of his arrived. But this was obviously not going to be enough. The man had plans to asphalt the lane to the side of the shop. He was chiding me about my over-modest plans – 'Think multi-storey', he intoned.

We all have our breaking point and mine came at the point when he was designing the swinging 'Valet Parking' sign. 'Can you just shut the f— up about parking for one tiny moment and think about food?' I pleaded. Guy looked hurt. I watched him get up, pocket his mobile phone, toss and catch his car keys, and exit with my hopes for £15,000. 'No vision,' he muttered, shaking his head wistfully.

The time had come to chat to my brother, and it was, as I had suspected, all too easy. He said he could lend me the purchase

21

price as a lump sum, which meant I would have just the sort of sizeable chunk that banks are willing to negotiate on. I don't of course mean the branch that had severed all links with me, but Simon's own local bank. We went to see them together the next morning, and they pledged to advance me an extra £10,000 as long as Simon left his building society book in their keeping as a guarantee.

This amazed me. If someone with a good banking history and a high income job could be treated with such suspicion, how do new account holders or recent immigrants ever get a loan? Do they chuck in body organs as a bit of extra collateral? Still, my own immediate worries were at an end. I had £25,000 to get my venture underway. It seemed to me an enormous sum, though of course it barely buys a shiny whisk once you start getting into commercial equipment. But it goes a fair way in acquiring secondhand restaurant gear, as I was planning to do.

My strategy was to throw all my money upfront where it was most visible, in a Blitzkrieg approach. If the business made money I would be alright, and if it didn't then nothing much would matter anyway. Cutting things down to a minimum, doing a lot of the refurbishment myself, I calculated that I would need £13,000 to get some food on the tables.

So I phoned Kevin and offered £12,000, saying that this was all I had; if it wasn't enough, then thanks anyway, I hoped they'd sell it soon. Kevin said he needed time to think. Within a week the estate agent got back to me, asking if I could stretch to £13,000? I said no, I really only had £12,000. Two hours later it was mine.

A bitter north wind funnelled along the high street, driving grit into my eyes and wrapping old crisp packets around my legs as I fought my way uphill from the estate agents with the keys to

Cain's in my pocket. I don't think I'd ever felt quite so cold or wretched before.

It wasn't that I expected marching bands and a handshake from the mayor, exactly, nor did I expect the estate agent to carry me over the threshold. But a tiny bit of sun or human warmth would have been nice. Clearly the commission on £12,000 isn't enormous. The estate agent had informed me rather perfunctorily that my funds hadn't yet been transferred into his account, and that I should come back a little later (ie wait outside in the freezing cold). I gave it ten minutes, then returned to disrupt his cosy little den by shivering uncontrollably and blowing into my palms. He reluctantly handed over the documents and steered me back into the cold.

I don't think the weather was entirely to blame for my dose of *tristesse*. The night before, I'd phoned Amanda to ask her along to the ceremonial handover and Guy had answered. He couldn't help but tell me about his great new start-up investment. Funky cobbling for driveways. The money was just flooding in.

A 'Sold' sign was flapping in the wind in front of Cain's so I ripped it off with frozen hands and hurled it down the muddy alleyway, where it caught on a discarded metal pole. Then I unlocked the door and, shoving aside a pile of junk mail, stepped inside. I walked slowly round looking at everything – the crockery, the tables, the equipment – nervous about touching it. It didn't feel like it was mine. In fact, it felt very much like trespassing.

I sat for a while on the little brick wall that Kevin had used as a bar and tried to envisage all the changes I'd make. Right, I thought, off we go. Two hours later I was still sitting on the wall, colder than ever, as I'd failed to work out the heating. But an idea had sprung to mind. Dragging the metal pole in from the alleyway, I practised swinging it over my head a few times and then brought it crashing down on the bar. An hour later, choking

23

on dust, with rivulets of grimy sweat running down my face, I looked happily down at a pile of broken bricks and debris. Yep, my diner was taking shape.

Mi casa, su casa

BEGINNING WORK ON THE DINER, chunks were soon getting whittled away from the log of my idealism. For example, I had never understood why shopfitters covered their windows with that smeary stuff to stop you looking in. Surely the innocent interest people have in a new shop should act as kindling in starting the hoped-for wildfire of publicity? At the Diner, therefore, I decided to invite in anyone who showed an interest, and share a cuppa or maybe a friendly glass of wine, *mi casa, su casa*, style. We could bat ideas around; I could ask their advice on how to reach out to the community, and they could tell me what they would like me to include on the menu.

As it turned out, as soon as people started looking in at me I became self-conscious and either waved them away (if they were kids), or adopted a foolish grin if dealing with adults. Some people continued staring, nonetheless, which occasionally drove me to hide behind things until they'd gone, or even pretend to walk down steps to a cellar, hidden behind some boxes. This wasn't too tricky; you just had to time the crouch right while edging forward as if descending. A minute or two with your head ducked down would suffice before the onlookers – as often as not twelve-year-olds intent on making 'wanker' signs – lost interest and drifted away.

One day, however, I emerged from my 'cellar' to find Kevin staring in surprise from the doorway. Kevin had never shown quite the same openness and trust since receiving my first offer on the place but now he seemed to have serious misgivings.

'You alright?' he asked, moving his eyes slowly from the boxes to me.

'Yes, fine,' I answered blithely, 'just having a sit and a... think, y'know... as you do.' It seemed to satisfy him.

'Fair enough', he replied. And then turning back with a broad grin on his face, 'Let me know if you find anything interesting in the attic, won't you, mate?'

I decided to cover up the windows, and set to working out how to do it. You see whited-out, midst-of-fitting windows all the time, but what are you supposed to use to create the effect? Some kind of cloudy compound obviously, but what? My brother-in-law suggested it might be Vaseline. 'That's it,' I said, and bought a couple of king-size tubs. Which was how I came to be standing in the restaurant, smearing the windows in front of a small crowd of schoolboys, when a confident-looking teenager roughly elbowed them out the way and walked in.

'What are you doing?' she said.

'Isn't it obvious?' I said. 'I'm lubricating my windows. Did you want something?'

'I was going to ask you for a job,' she replied, 'but now I'm not so sure.'

Becky was pretty, with a freckly face and piles and piles of frizzy red hair, which she tied out of the way with a thick band.

For those who remember children's television of the 1970s, she faintly resembled Crystal Tipps, from *Crystal Tipps and Alistair*, only a less flakey version. She was the sort of girl who you would be happy to have babysit your kids (and your kids would love as a babysitter), at least until you met her older and scarier boyfriend. She claimed to be seventeen but eventually owned up to being sixteen, just – well, sixteen in a few weeks' time, more or less.

I pointed out that employing under-sixteens is a pain in the neck – too many rules and regulations and, besides, we were licensed, which made it illegal. Becky took it all in good part, then suggested that I use a watered-down white emulsion on the windows instead of the Vaseline. Clever. She offered to help me get the Vaseline off and, when the twelve-year-olds returned, popped outside to cuff them round the ear.

As we de-lubed, Becky explained that her mother had gone to live with her boyfriend in Crawley, leaving her the council house. Her own boyfriend, Lee, had moved in and was 'doing her head in', which was why she needed to get out for a couple of evenings a week. If we let her start at the Diner she wouldn't be in the way at all and wouldn't touch even a drop of alcohol. I found myself agreeing that she could pop in from time to time, but not in the evenings or school hours until her birthday. Then she'd be on the team.

With the demolition work almost completed I began to put some serious thought into refurbishing and decorating the place. Now, people have very fixed ideas about diners. They always picture that sparkly chrome 1950s look when, in fact, diners were supposed to be functional, clean and modern places for people to go and dine in. To restrict them to a particular retro 'look' was like saying that any 'restaurant' had to be French and from the *fin de siècle* Moulin Rouge era of candlesticks and red flocked wallpaper. Obviously a daft idea.

For months I had been gathering design ideas together, cutting pictures out of magazines and buying fantastically expensive restaurant design books from America. While I was quite happy to plunder ideas from classic venues like the City Bakery in New York or The Louisiana Grill in Memphis, my instincts were set against a pastiche-y *Happy Days* style. Obviously, the seats would be set into booths and upholstered in deep-red leatherette, and the tables would have marbley Formica tops, but that was about as far as I'd go. There'd be no jukeboxes on the tables (couldn't afford them), no girls in pink dresses whizzing round on roller skates (why give it all away on accident insurance?), and no Buddy Holly either (much prefer Elvis).

While mulling over the final scheme for the decor, a succession of shopfitters arrived to offer professional guidance. Each one leafed through my design idea scrapbooks, raised admiring eyebrows at the cuttings and cross-references, muttering, 'Yep, yep. Got that, very nice. A-ha, no problem,' then looked up blankly and asked, 'So, what will it be then: Fifties *Happy Days* look?' A week later I would get a quote roughly equivalent to the GDP of Norway.

It was obvious that I was going to have to think laterally and look for a gifted, reasonably cheap, handyman to take on the job. Myself, for instance. Except that I'm no DIY expert (I blame the tools) and within a week I was at A&E getting a dressing for a hacked finger. This actually proved a lucky turn, as the nurse who filled out the injury questionnaire happened to have a master builder for a dad and, though he was retired, she thought he'd be quite happy to knock up some tables and a counter for me. Her husband, by an amazing coincidence, was a builder's mate and just happened to be looking for a job as well.

28

The following day, at 8am sharp, a neat-looking man with trimmed grey hair stood waiting outside the Diner. His name was Ken, and beside him, shivering and with the hood of his sweatshirt pulled over his head, was André, his unemployed son-in-law from Dieppe. Over the next three weeks the top of the High Street rang to the happy sound of the two men working hard, sawing, hammering and planing, and of me boiling the kettle and pouring them tea.

Ken proved to be the kind of competent, kindly older man that we all need to have living round the corner. He didn't tell me how to design my diner; just looked at the pictures and said, 'Yeah, I can do that,' and then began measuring up. André's job was to fetch and carry. At the start of the day Ken would patiently explain to him what he needed from the hardware store and off he'd go. Half an hour later he would return with an item so entirely wide of the mark we couldn't understand how he could even have considered it (think towel-ring instead of dowelling and you get the drift). Ken would then painstakingly run through the list again, perhaps throwing in some mime to help matters along. I can only imagine the fun those smug patronising bastards in our local hardware store were having. (Two years later they had scared off so many customers they were forced to close. Well, *quel dommage!*)

There was nothing for it but for André and I to swap jobs and, in doing so, a great mystery was explained. As young teenagers, an elderly aunt had taken my brother and I out to lunch in Littlehampton. At the end of the meal the French waiter, without any provocation or lead-up, leant across my aunt's seat and told us both to fuck off. 'Fuck off, you,' he said, in a calm, matter-of-fact tone as if said on a daily basis to all the English customers. Auntie seemed oblivious, but my brother and I were stunned, far too nervous to draw her attention to this astonishing insult. Now, twenty years later, it happened again as André turned to

29

me and, with a note of inexplicable enquiry in his voice, said, 'Fuck off, you?' I gasped and stared. André looked confused. 'Ken ees 'avin coffeh,' he explained; then slightly more hesitantly, 'F'coffe you, too?' So, at long last I could stop feeling tense around French people.

With Ken's help and lots more hot drinks and expletives from André, the Diner began to take shape. Expertly crafted, wood-panelled booths sprung up, each one with a customised table at the centre edged in stainless steel. The walls were half-panelled and half-painted with emulsion and the floor was covered in green and white tiles in a checkerboard pattern with blue tiles round the sides. The latter I did myself and, though Ken winced slightly and sucked air through his teeth, I could tell he was just a tiny bit impressed.

It was remarkable, given the very few concessions we'd made to the 1950s look, just how much like a classic diner it was turning out. The bulkhead wall lamps set a pool of light sparkling on the Formica and spilling onto the shiny red leatherette seats, and there was an air of clean, shiny efficiency about the place that almost compelled you to slide into one of the booths and order some food. Or might have done, if I'd sorted out some kitchen equipment to cook it with. I was beginning to worry that my strategy of entirely ignoring the small kitchen tucked away in a room at the back, and throwing all the money at the seating area out front, might have been a bit misguided.

Kitchen design matters, as any caterer will tell you, and especially so in tiny restaurants where profits depend on getting people in and out as quickly as possible. McDonald's, Burger King, KFC, they all know this and put plenty of money into getting the perfect juxtaposition of grills, fryers and worktops, as their customers are paying for speed and consistency, not tasteful fittings or chic ambience. They also, of course, have ways of discouraging people from sitting endlessly over their polystyrene packages: using a mixture of bright lighting, seats angled just a tiny bit and Muzak playing on a loop that repeats subliminally the words 'Clear off we hate you' (okay, I made that last bit up). I was looking to be rather more welcoming than that but to keep the food moving in a similarly slick fashion, and there was only one way I could remotely achieve this – with a smart, efficient, totally redesigned kitchen. Well, that was the idea. A cheap makeover was about the best I could stretch to.

In the first days of feverish activity I had chucked out all the old pans and utensils, because using someone else's old pans feels a bit like wearing their old pants. This left me with only a couple of fridges and a cooker. Fridges are there just to keep food cold and as they were out of sight of the customer I refused to be seduced by the gleam of stainless steel or the satisfying velvety clunk of a new fridge door. The cooker, however, was another case entirely. Kevin had left an enormous old-fashioned range that looked like something Mrs Bridges might have used. It was made of iron and white enamel, so squat and so heavy it had its own special concrete plinth, with a capacious oven, six burners on top and a giant eye-level grill. All that's fine, but entirely unsuitable for the kind of food you serve in a diner, and it knew it, eyeing me like a fat albino toad, daring me to have a go.

Generally my way of dealing with really big problems is to ignore them until an even bigger problem comes along, at which point the original problem seems to fade away of its own accord. It's a technique worthy of a bestseller manual, and one I can't recommend highly enough, though there is a downside. You can find yourself jerking awake in the middle of the night and screaming out things like, 'So how am I going to cook the burgers, then? Boil them?'

31

At Hotelympia I had looked at beautifully designed and engi-
neered Italian cooking ranges, created from rich alloys
combined with thick chunky stainless steel, with no gaps for
things to fall down or food to get trapped, with low-slung,
streamlined, computer-aided controls set at a racey angle and
internal lighting, like the dashboard of a very, very expensive
sports car. These were the Ferraris of cooking equipment and I'd
stared at them like a small boy at the window of a car showroom.
Back at the Diner, I was saddled with a rattling old dormobile,
propped up on some bricks.

One day André sawed through a power cable and we were
without electricity. I tried to cope without coffee, but after half
an hour I could take it no longer. I filled a milk saucepan with
water and gingerly lit the gas and set it on the range. The water
seemed to cook quite well and before long we were all enjoying
a hearty cup of Nescafé and I felt ready to take a next step, with
toasted teacakes. Again, the range met the challenge. Now there
was no stopping me. Soup, French toast, baked potatoes, boil-in-
a-bag fish – I could cook it all. I couldn't understand why I'd
been so standoffish; soon the range and I were like old mates.

I set about designing the rest of the kitchen for maximum
ergonomic efficiency. The staff budget only allowed for one chef,
so the kitchen would have to fit him or her (or, more probably,
me) like a second skin. I bought a new chip fryer at an auction,
but that of course wouldn't help me cook burgers; I could hardly
deep-fry them. I jokingly asked Ken if he could knock me up a
griddle, and the next day he gave me a piece of paper with the
plans to give to a blacksmith. It was shockingly simple: the
blacksmith just cut out a square sheet of metal and we stuck it
over the gas burners on the range.

The time had come to cook some diner food. I bought some
organic mince from a local butcher and moulded and bashed it
into rough burger shapes. Meanwhile Ken and André poured the

beer and laid the table, or at least moved some of the sawdust out of the way. I lit the gas burners underneath the metal plate, and we were off.

The home-made griddle got hot, got very hot, turned purple, smoked and then folded up like an origami tulip. I put the burgers on anyway but they immediately stuck to the metal and gave off a searing stench of burnt protein reminiscent of nastier incidents at the dentist's. Never mind, I chiselled away until the burgers came away from the metal (you're supposed to 'seal the meat' anyway, so that was alright), put the buns in to toast, and organised the salady stuff for underneath the meat. The fat from the burgers collected in the channel where the griddle surface was listing at an alarming angle and, as I lifted one side of the griddle to pour it off, I managed to tip it into the flames, where it combusted spectacularly, spitting oil over my hands and making my eyes water. In the excitement I forgot the buns under the grill, which were burning merrily, their smoke billowing through the restaurant. It was all quite exhilarating – men's work. Flames, hot metal, sweat, fear. I felt like Casey Jones.

André had requested his burger rare, but even he was surprised at just how rare it was once you got through the hard black crust on the outside. Ken asked if I'd ever done any cooking before and wondered if he might have another beer.

Still, the first burgers had been served at the Diner, and it seemed a pretty emotional moment. Or was that just the smoke getting in my eyes?

33

The trial run had thrown up some interesting discussion points. Fortunately, indeed miraculously, the griddle plate went back to its normal shape when it cooled down a bit, and I took it back to the blacksmith to get a grease channel put in. Further trials showed that by controlling the heat a bit better I could keep it flat. The performance of the home-made burgers was slightly more of a worry but there was plenty of time to experiment. I pushed it to the back of my mind in order to concentrate on more crucial stuff, like what pictures to put up.

On this score, there seemed no harm in going to the professionals, so I looked in at a swish Brighton poster shop, where I was taken upstairs to their corporate art department. After several days of extensive research they suggested Edward Hopper and recommended that I buy from them several hundred pounds' worth of prints featuring pictures of people sitting in diners. 'Correct me I'm wrong,' I said, 'but isn't Hopper's work noted for its depiction of loneliness and isolation? Would anyone want to sit in a diner and look at lonely people sitting in diners? Might depressed people think we were taking the piss?'

Had they been looking for the very least suitable artist they couldn't have done better. It was a bit like suggesting Munch's *The Scream* as a nice, soothing print for a psychiatric hospital. Anyway, an unexpected bill from the extractor fan people meant that I had to scale down my plans. Instead I cobbled together montages from old postcards, books and magazines and placed them artily about the walls in clipframes. One can worry about the look of things too much.

One cannot, however, worry too much about a name, and although the diner concept was becoming reality before my eyes, I still had not decided what to call the place.

34

I'm convinced that two simple words is more than sufficient for a restaurant name – and all the better if one of them is 'The'. I was once interviewed by The Great American Deep Pan Pizza Company. Well, that's just crap, isn't it? And for a while I worked for Pastificio, which is Italian for 'pasta factory' – very apt and good because we made our own pasta, but very bad because people were frightened about saying it wrong. 'Let's go to Pastifishio... pastifickio... pastaaa... oh sod it, let's go to Pizza Express.' (It was pasti-feetch-ee-o.)

But perhaps Italian names are a problem, as all too many descend into initials. I won't go to ASK for oh so many reasons, but primarily because they have such a dumb name. And the same applies big time to ITS, Si, Est and – I can hardly type it – NTI (Now That's Italian!). These aren't names so much as clever ways to use up your last Scrabble letters.

I was still doing occasional shifts as a room service waiter while planning the Diner, and I put my shortlist of names into a little competition at the hotel. The names were listed on a large piece of paper and fellow staff were invited to vote for their favourite, or to suggest their own, the winners getting a free slap-up meal when we opened.

The list went:

The Big Diner (because it was very small, ho ho ho)
Pig Heaven
Burger Express (well, why not?)
Cheap'n'Greasy
Maximum Diner
Eat Up Rodney! (in homage to *Get Dressed Rodney!*, a clothes shop in Camden)

I forget which option was the most popular – I think it was 'Pig Heaven' – as I gave my own nomination, a large block vote that carried the day, for 'Maximum Diner'. You need to be careful with competitions, anyway. Whenever I go back to my mum's home in Henfield, I walk past a lovely, classy gift shop, the owners of which put its naming out to a very public competition in the local paper and somehow wound up with 'Top Shelf'. It can't just be me who's reminded by this of adult only mags or the place where you hide unwanted presents.

35

During the 1980s the brave people at 'I Can't Believe It's Not Butter' liberated forever the naming of products. This was such a seismic shift in naming that I brought samples home from America to show incredulous friends and family long before it was available here. My mother insisted on calling it 'Let's Pretend It's Butter!', which seemed even more surreal. But now any old marketing department thinks it can give a product a crazily honest name. Sometimes it works, such as the American removal company 'Two Jewish Guys with a Truck', and sometimes it can be frankly misguided: Safeway's 'Don't Flutter with the Butter!' means what exactly? A soft spread for cardiac patients?

'Maximum Diner', by contrast, was a clear winner. If you want to get technical, it was a combination of two naming techniques: firstly, finding a word that sounds effective, in this case maximum; and secondly, going for a slightly unsettling weirdness. But the main thing was that it just sounded right, while the rest of that shortlist – well, it speaks for itself.

It's the menu, stupid

BACK IN THE KITCHEN TIME WAS PRESSING ON and the Menu had become Worry #1. Borrowing from Bill Clinton's technique for concentrating the mind, I wrote, 'It's the Menu, Stupid' on the wall – but then ignored it. Meanwhile, the interior had pretty much come together, the liquor licence was transferred from a much happier, slimmer Kevin (the change was remarkable, but I was far too preoccupied to draw any lessons from it), opening day bunting had been ordered, and I'd even had some T-shirts printed for the staff with the logo 'Maximum Diner–Somewhere to Eat'. A snappy bit of advertising, to be sure, but to eat what? That was my problem.

Burgers, obviously. But even this staple was proving difficult to get hold of. I'd assumed when I'd planned the Diner that I could order organic or free range beef and chicken burgers, frozen, individually wrapped and ready to be flipped onto the griddle. How wrong could I have been? Extensive research and frustrated phone calls to the RSPCA, Compassion in World Farming and People for the Ethical Treatment of Animals all confirmed that there were no business-scale suppliers of free range pre-prepared meat. My only option was to find a decent farmer with a healthy, happy herd, negotiate a deal and then make the burgers myself. From my trial run I knew this would be disastrous. Ready-made burgers are flattened into thin round shapes so they seal and cook quickly and tend not to either fall apart or spit runnels of fat that burst into flames. But the only ready-made burgers, bacon or chicken products came from the standard suppliers, who could offer no comfort about how their meat was reared or processed.

A dark night of the soul followed this discovery. You see, I'm a special kind of vegetarian, the kind that eats meat. I know that sounds bizarre but just because I suspect that killing animals is wrong (though what's supposed to happen to all those dairy herds and shorn sheep, I can't imagine) doesn't mean I'm ready for a lifetime commitment to nut roasts and lentil lasagne. What I care about is that the meat I eat has had some chance of a happy life (okay, until the point when it gets strung up, amateurishly stunned and has its throat cut).

The question was, could I give up that last shred of principle and collude with factory farming, just to keep a business going; just to preserve myself from hideous debt and the humiliation of failing before I'd even started? Well, put like that, yes, perhaps I could. But to salve my conscience I decided that I'd buy the best quality meat I could afford, in the hopes that the animals had suffered less. (Obviously, once my franchise was up and running I could set up my own supplies.) At the same time I'd offer menu alternatives that would be tasty, innovative and not made of beef. But what? The question was starting to get repetitive.

I did have a few favourite recipes that I'd picked up through the years: my mother's lamb and apricot pie, flapjacks, Josceline Dimbleby's bacon and cheese hotpot, to name but three (in fact to name all three). But there was no unifying theme, no new concept for customers to grasp. On the other hand, I did have a few buccaneering ideas about language. 'Cheese', for instance, could be used as a verb, as well as a noun. The staff would say, 'Would you like that cheesed, madam?' or 'Cheese it up for you, sir?' or 'Hey sonny, bet you'd like me to cheese that!'

I even explored the idea of adapting the French word for cheese, *fromage*, into an English verb, to *frommage*, pronunciation similar to 'rummage', meaning 'to add cheese to something'. But my computer kept writing a squiggly red line under frommage (it's done it again), suggesting that we'd got a way to go with that one. Ambitious? Perhaps. But one day long ago, at a meeting of McDonald's executives, someone must have had the courage to say, 'Hey guys, you know those kids' meals? Well, I've been thinking, let's call them Happy Meals!' And I bet someone else at the table sniggered, and thanked Christ he hadn't come up with such a stupid idea himself.

I'm not a chef, as might be clear by now. Chefs cook proper food in restaurants; they are alert to bold new combinations of flavour and texture; they like to make witty allusions to other dishes; and they speak their own language (French, mainly), bandying about such words as *soufflé, truffle oil, calves' liver, praline, jus, tatin, celeriac, flaaaaaan, confit*. Few of these filtered through to me at my course at Leeds Poly, where, to be fair, they weren't actually trying to turn out chefs so much as managers with academic qualifications – not a thing you boast about in the hot, bitchy, competitive world of commercial kitchens, although the worlds aren't always as far apart as they seem.

For instance, one visiting lecturer was keen to impress upon us how important it was to judge the market accurately when you're setting a menu. As an example, he cited the case of an ambitious young chef from the Yorkshire Dales who had trained at the Académie de Très Bien Cuisine in Paris during the glory days of *nouvelle cuisine*. Having patiently learned his craft from the very best, suffering diabolical mockery from his Gallic colleagues before finally earning their respect, he returned home to show Yorkshire how it should be eating. His business lasted for three sad, argumentative months. As the bailiffs chucked his exquisite restaurant furniture in the back of a lorry, the young chef complained that the people of Yorkshire didn't understand that truly great food takes a lot longer to produce, that portions were supposed to be small, that was the bloody point of them, and that he felt very, very disappointed in everyone. He left catering quite soon afterwards and has hardly cooked since. 'I know this,' our lecturer informed us, shooting the cuffs of his frayed corduroy jacket, and staring at each row in turn, 'because I was that young chef...'

Fortunately for me, diner cooking requires a more simple style – one that, like peasant or café food, is based around cheap, fresh ingredients. This was good, because it's the kind of food I know best; no cause for any shame about that, as anyone going into business should know their strengths and limitations, and have clear goals in mind. Mine was to make money and provide a great service, not to push the envelope when it comes to what you can do with a monkfish.

40   My menu research might not have uncovered any great new culinary ideas, but it crystallised the huge changes that have happened with food in my lifetime. As recently as the 1970s, getting a 'balanced diet' meant eating enough of the basic five food groups (protein, carbohydrate, fats/oils, vegetables and the other one) to avoid a deficiency that could lead to rickets, beriberi, scurvy and so on. Now, when dieticians suggest we eat a balanced diet they are pleading with us not to get any fatter. It's a subtle change.

Five new food groups have now taken their place. At #1, still, is the cheap filling carbohydrate (pasta, bread, potatoes, pastry), and at #2 protein (meat, chicken or fish), more or less of it according to whether times are good or bad. But, while in the old days we would then have a veg or two, in the modern western world we now pass on this because they don't taste particularly nice and are annoying to prepare. Instead at #3 we have topping, which may but by no means has to be a vegetable (usually onion or mushroom, never pea or sprout); it can equally be another protein, like cheese or bacon, or – my favourite – both. This new food group is responsible for many of the world's problems, among them obesity, heart disease, cancer, piles (apparently) and road rage (arguably). Meanwhile, in at #4 is the tangy sauce: barbecue, blue cheese, thousand island, whatever – nutritionally worthless but lovely. And at #5 is side salad, including its sub-sets of garnish, coleslaw and, debatably, potato salad.

So, planning a menu for the Maximum Diner was actually quite simple. I just needed to find the most popular items in each of these five core categories – carbohydrate, protein, topping, tangy sauce and side salad – and there it was. The menu had almost written itself.

There is, though, a second principle to keep in mind: that nearly everything would have to be edible by hand while driving or watching telly, or at the very least one-handed with a fork, without looking at it (so one can still watch the TV/road). Snobs who dismiss such considerations might want to recall that the inventor of convenience food was the Earl of Sandwich. Not being minded to leave the gambling table, and wanting a food-stuff that he could hold without getting his playing cards greasy, the good Earl asked his servants for meat wrapped in bread.

Virtually every fast food item has to satisfy the requirement of not getting the steering wheel greasy, or not requiring cutting up for children, and those that don't have lost out to those that do.

Thus the revival of Kentucky Fried Chicken came about only when Colonel Sanders realised that his secret recipe was all very well, but what people wanted was cheap chicken products that could be easily held – chicken burgers, wraps, twisters – instead of those bony quarters of chicken that were difficult, hot and messy to hold in your hands.

In fact, the recipe for fast food is pretty much written in stone: a nice moist protein wrapped in a nice dry carbohydrate filled with a nice bit of topping for added value and something nice and tangy for flavour. The salad is integrated (for example, in burgers), or optional.

Although it didn't quite follow these rules to the letter, one idea I wanted to develop and popularise was *hash*. There's nothing new in food – I nicked the idea myself from a little café in Brighton, although I believe corned beef hash is a northern delicacy. It also appears in the chefs' bible, the *Larousse Gastronomique*, as a French dish, *hachis*, which uses leftovers in a stir-fry with potatoes. Everyone loves fried potatoes: Belgians like them with mayonnaise on them, the Swiss make them into complicated little cakes called *rosti*, and so do Americans but they call them hash browns.

Hash, or *hachis*, puts them in a stir-fry context. What you do is, you get some leftovers. You chop those and then fry them with some other leftovers. You toss in some leftover potatoes, also chopped up, fry them all up and add something (possibly something left over) to make the whole lot taste nice. Of course we were going to do it on a commercial scale not using leftovers (I emphasise NOT USING LEFTOVERS), but that's the general idea. It's nicer than it sounds, is enormously adaptable, can be eaten with a fork, needn't be cut up for children and is dead cheap. It is hot, fast, filling and economical. You can luxury-it-up or cheapen-it-down, cheese-it, *frommage*-it even, slather-it (another word I was trying to repopularise) in any sauce you can

42

think of, and adapt it for any culture, adding goat, say for Iraq, or extra potato for Ireland. It's a wonder food.

I was concerned that it might be difficult to sell the concept of hash to the people of Uckfield, or, worse, that it would be mistaken for its dopey namesake, but I took comfort from the development of Chinese food in this country. That must have been a tricky proposition to sell. When the Chinese started arriving, how many of us had tried or even heard of their food? I suspect they won us over with one entry-level dish that people simply couldn't resist: sweet'n'sour. It doesn't appear on any menus in China, so they must have inscrutably invented an item specifically to appeal to a western palate.

Then, in the late 1980s, as sweet'n'sour became slightly naff, and the Thais started setting up shop, stealing customers away with green curry, the Chinese came back with another humdinger and, guess what, it was fun for kids and you could eat it with your hands. crispy aromatic duck: a moist protein (duck) wrapped in a nice dry carbohydrate (pancake) with an oh-so-tangy sauce (hoi sin) and a topping/side salad combined in cucumber and spring onion. It was a work of genius; only the Chinese, the inventors of gunpowder, could devise so fiendishly clever a dish to see off the Thais. Now they just need to adapt it for driving.

With staples established, the remaining problem was to come up with a 'signature dish'. Marco Pierre White has his Omelette Arnold Bennett, Escoffier had his Peach Melba, McDonald's have their Big Mac, and Burger King their Whopper. I needed something of similar class for Maximum Diner. My favourite foods are cheese, bacon and barbecue sauce so it wasn't difficult. Any item with those three things on it would be given the sobriquet 'Maximum' or 'Max', and would be our signature dishes. The Big Max, for example, a quarterpounder burger with cheese and bacon and barbecue sauce on top and salad and mayo below, would be our very own Big Mac, all set for a nicely publicised

43

'McPassing off' court battle with you know who (which unfortunately never happened). The Maximum Chicken Dinner would be a griddled chicken breast generously cheesed-up and slathered in bacon, nestling on a bed of chips with barbecue sauce and coleslaw on the side. Maximum Hash was stir-fried onion, bacon, mushroom and peppers, plus potatoes frommaged and grilled until nicely brown, served with side salad and a dip (barbecue).

Apart from the twelve different variations on hash, the rest of the menu was made up of standards: there's little point in being very creative with fast food due to Pareto's Law. This rule, devised by Vilfredo Pareto, a nineteenth-century Italian economist, states that 80 percent of x comes from 20 percent of y. Pareto used his theory as an argument against socialism, citing evidence that (whatever political system was in place) 20 percent of the population always took 80 percent of the income. In my context, it meant that 20 percent of customers would produce 80 percent of turnover, and also that 20 percent of my menu would produce 80 percent of my orders. In short, a small number of regulars ordering a limited selection of items were going to be the making or breaking of the Diner.

It also meant that there was no need to hum and hah endlessly about, say, what drinks to serve – should we go for that range of flavoured fizzy waters or not? – because almost everyone is going to order the Coke, Diet Coke or beer (so make sure you're well stocked on those and have set the price carefully). The same will be true of your wine list, as 80 percent of the customers will order from 20 percent of the wines, whether that's the house wine or the second cheapest (which is the one I always go for).

Of course, Pareto's Law isn't to be confused with Potatoes Law, which states that 80 percent of your profits come from potato.

Having more or less established the basics I would need, in the way of drinks, canned food and sauces, I took myself off to Booker Cash and Carry in Brighton.

Booker's is a vast warehouse the size of two or three football pitches, with pallets stacked five high and forklift trucks gliding around silently on the polished concrete floor. The first time I got past security and in through the main set of doors (they don't just let anyone in), I was slack-jawed with amazement and had to almost stop myself shouting, 'JESUS H. CHRIST! WOULD YOU LOOK AT ALL THAT FOOD!'

I could imagine warehouses like this on far-off planets keeping colonies going for years and, as if to bolster the science fiction fantasy, the place seemed peopled by androids: busy, unsmiling characters whisking up and down the aisles, picking what they needed with mechanical efficiency. Only occasionally were these impressions broken, by a huddle of Asian shopkeepers chatting animatedly at an aisle corner, or a cash'n'carry virgin wandering around bewildered with one or two sample packs rattling around in a vast trolley.

At the till I bumped into an old catering friend, who told me that his Brighton hotel was hosting that year's Fast Food Fair and suggested I dropped by for some culinary inspiration and sample eats. 'It'll be the cheapest and best buffet in town,' he enthused. He wasn't wrong. The next day I joined the crowds shouldering their way through a vast hotel lobby and hall, packed with stalls from food manufacturers. There must have been hundreds of them and they were all offering free samples of their products, from burgers to biscuits, by way of an almost endless variety of deep-fried potato.

After a couple of hours of gamely sampling samples, I was too stuffed to talk sensibly with sales reps, so I joined some old hotel acquaintances at the bar and then decided to lie on the beach for a while.

45

In the end I had to make three visits on consecutive days to sample everything. This was only partly gluttony. There's an etiquette to be observed at these sort of events, for, while Pareto's Law shows people want the same few products, as we've seen from the Chinese there are world-beating new food ideas out there, waiting to be discovered. Hence each supplier feels duty-bound to invent new, exciting products.

As a rookie I got ensnared in a too-long conversation with a beautiful rep promoting tandoori-flavour fries as the next big thing. I suggested it might be better to have potato flavour 'chips' that customers could dip in tandoori sauce as and when required, but she looked at me blankly and said, 'Yes, but these have *integral* tandoori. The flavour is actually *inside* the fry!'

'I understand,' I replied, 'but why do that? I mean, why bother?' Someone had to ask the question.

'Because, it's like... the tandoori is within the fry, right? It's a whole, new, concept, in... FRIES.' She pronounced quite slowly.

'Yes, but... what was wrong with the old concept?' I asked.

'Look, I'm just trying to sell chips,' she snapped, suddenly looking very tired. 'If you don't want them, then sod off.'

That I could relate to. In an impulsive act of solidarity I bought four boxes. They stayed in a freezer for the next couple of years until we ran out of chips one night and they saved the day. Hurrah for innovation!

Now that I had the menu and the food costs sorted, it was time to start setting the prices. There are various mechanisms for doing this, but in general the rule is to take the total cost of the food, multiply it by three (to cover overheads) plus a tiny bit (your profit) and then add VAT. I did this for each product and then said, 'Bloody hell, I can't charge that!' Reverting to the 'slightly cheaper than everyone else' method, I quickly sent the menus off to the printers. I was starting to get fed up with all the preparation and wanted to start serving customers.

As well as the popularisation of hash, rewriting the language of food and bringing fast food know-how to the provinces, our other USP (Unique Selling Point) was our direct approach to describing our dishes. I simply don't believe you should burden customers with too much information about their food, and have a pet theory that the posher the restaurant, the less appetising the food, because they will insist on listing every single ingredient. For example, at a London gastropub I was recently offered 'Walnut sourdough cake with apricot compote and orange curd ice cream'. Now, I was more than happy with the cake, walnut and ice cream elements; reasonably okay with the apricot, a bit suspicious of the sourdough, but I didn't fancy that curd at all, so no thanks.

Another familiar tactic is to give the food a sort of mini-CV. We all know what garlic bread is, for instance. But do customers need to read that they'll be getting 'Three pieces of locally baked French stick, carefully sliced by Raul, drenched in garlic butter and fresh herbs, then lightly toasted and served in a little basket. We think it's the best in town. Enjoy!'? I doubt it, and they'll never, *ever* get back the 4.5 seconds it takes to read all that. So our food descriptions were going to be a model of brevity and clarity: cheeseburger, bacon sandwich – simplicity itself.

At the same time, however, I recognised that people often don't want to talk while out for a meal with their significant other, but feel it's rude to open a paper. To provide entertainment to these people, we put a few comments on the back of the menu:

YOU NEED THE MAXIMUM DINER BECAUSE:
We put the urge back into burgers, whatever that means.
We named a burger after you.

It's more than a fastfood restaurant, there's a payphone too.
We're open 'til midnight, so you can come in when you're
    rat-arsed!
If you don't come in we'll close down and you'll have to go
    back to Starburger.
Our staff are polite and welcoming and one of them once did
    a catering course.
We don't know the meaning of gristle.

PRESS REACTION TO THE MAXIMUM DINER:

'Better napkins than at Burger King.' What Takeaway
'Succulent, moist meat, and that's just the staff.' Snack!
'We were impressed by the friendly staff. Mind you, we don't
    get out much.' East Sussex Caterer
'These guys don't know the meaning of botulism.' Restaurant
Hygiene Quarterly

My sister-in-law vetoed *Our burgers are only made from criminal cows who deserved to die* on the grounds that it might frighten the children, while Becky felt that the phrase *You can come in when you're rat-arsed!* was a bit superfluous in Uckfield, as most of our customers would be anyway. I remember chuckling indulgently when she said that, so that she wouldn't feel her joke had fallen flat. Unfortunately, as it turned out, she was rather downplaying the problem.

That same week the new sign arrived, and in an emotional little ceremony Ken and André stood on ladders fixing it to the wall while I yelled up at them from the road, 'Left a bit, no right a bit, no hang on...' and Becky brought out a tray of celebratory coffees and biscuits. The four of us stood around in the chilly April wind, clinking mugs together and staring complacently as the glimmering sunshine bounced off the burnished metal. The countdown to opening had begun. All we needed were a few final bits of snagging on the building works. And some staff.

We are Family

THERE'S A SCENE IN *THE ENFORCER* where Detective Inspector Harry 'Dirty Harry' Callaghan is very cross indeed. His partner's been iced (again!) and Harry is out for revenge against the punks who did it. But the DA's had it with violent mavericks in his department and informs him he's being transferred to the personnel department. 'Personnel?' exclaims our hero, looking at his boss incredulously, 'but that's for assholes.'

Well, Mr Harold Callaghan! I may not know a whole lot about policing the mean streets of LA, but I do know that you'd soon find yourself in a pretty pickle without those assholes to pick up after you – organising funerals, new partner induction, a bit of positive feedback, not to mention a nice new uniform when you've just been shot! These things don't just sort themselves out on their own. I should know because I have to do the work those assholes do, without any back-up from a slick, professionally trained department. And, as any independent trader will tell you, organising staff is the world's biggest headache. Why? Because it's one of your biggest expenses and, unlike food supplies and fixed costs like rent (which are, erm, fixed), it's the only one you'll be able to cut when times get hard. Though, even when times are good, staffing is a never-ending worry.

Labour is also the business input most likely to go wrong. Ovens can blow up, suppliers can forget to deliver, rivers can overflow and send five foot of sewage through your dining area (as we'll see in a later chapter), but at six o'clock on a Friday evening, when the phone rings, it's not going to be any of those things, but the mother of your number one waitress calling to say that she's not been feeling well all day and really shouldn't work around food tonight. What does the manager have to do then? He or she has to plead and beg and cajole and bribe the other staff. So you see, Harry – you'd better choose who you work with carefully and treat them well.

On the whole the catering industry doesn't. With its crummy pay, poor conditions and marginal security, the system tends to exploit the large numbers of people who simply can't find other paid work or who have to fit a job around their family or other commitments. In theory, 'the market' will sort it all out, ensuring that those companies that pay the worst will get the worst employees and so lose customers to those that employ the best staff by paying the best wages. But you could wait forever for that to happen and, as Winston Churchill (never I suspect a member of the Low Pay Unit) said in 1906: 'Bad employers must be made to pay a decent wage to prevent them from undercutting the good ones.'

During the infamous 'McLibel' trial, when a couple of British anarchists took on Corporate USA, McDonald's were accused of forcing down wages across the industry. However, in my experience it is the independent traders who are most likely to be shamelessly ripping off their staff. Large companies have professional human resources managers looking after staff affairs, and they know more than anyone that workers have ways of fighting back against bad employers. Which makes being a good employer simply better business. Human resources managers go even further, advancing the idea that professional, dedicated management create an efficient, loyal staff who have a family identification with their company, while weak, shifty management get liberty-taking shysters. Well, maybe.

I was determined, in any case, to be an intelligent, modern manager, getting the best out of my workforce – sorry, family – by fostering an idea that we were a genuine team, striving to do something great for Uckfield. Blue-skies thinking or a load of old cobblers? The proof of the pudding would be in the baking.

Amidst the hubbub of electricians reconnecting the power, Ken finishing off the counter, and André holding things, I tried to conduct staff interviews.

During my Wilderness Years of taking any old shift work in the catering trade, I'd attended an interview or two and knew a little about how they should be conducted. Basically, you make them as scientific as possible, with specific questions to ascertain specific points, and a progression that moves neatly from area to area, while cross-referencing to look for inconsistencies (lies); then you throw in a couple of open-ended questions to discover how interesting the applicant is. What you shouldn't do is pour the applicant a large coffee and say, 'Okay, so tell me all about yourself?' For one, the applicant has to finish the coffee, leaving agonies of silent slurping long after they've disclosed to you that they don't really like working with people and prefer chatting to the colonies of E. coli they keep in Petri dishes under the bed, or burbling on about the high cost of imported pornography.

51

Worse still is when employers just grab the limelight and drone on about themselves and their hopes for the business.

I was determined to avoid these pitfalls and take a proper, fair, organised approach. Then Marti, a handsome woman in her mid-thirties, popped her head round the door and asked if we might need an assistant manager. She'd heard about the vacancy through Becky and, as she'd had loads of experience of working in cafés and restaurants, and was incredibly flexible about the hours she could work, she thought she should apply. There was something about Marti's crinkly smile and sympathetic manner – the way she fussed over my multiple burns and injuries, and tutted when I said I didn't have a girlfriend (as if she knew where likely candidates were right now forming an orderly queue) – that was appealing. Though dressed in a suit for the occasion, she had a reassuring Earth Motherliness about her that I felt would be an asset. It was only after she'd left (with an agreement that she would start the following week as she was a bit tied up right now), that I began to wonder precisely where it was she had worked, and whether she hadn't just slightly overestimated her availability. Oh well, it doesn't do to pry too much.

For waitering jobs I had dozens of applicants. Becky seemed to know everyone in the town and yelled out comments as I went through the names. They were mainly unhelpful ones, along the lines of, 'No! Bitch!', 'No! Slag!', 'No! Brainiac!', though when I interviewed the youths they seemed perfectly okay and neither 'completely up themselves' or to 'think they were all that', as Becky had intimated. I finally settled on Catherine, a sixteen-year-old with catering experience, who seemed a calm and highly competent person.

The countdown to opening had begun. In fact, we had just two weeks left. So the idea was that Marti and Catherine would begin practising with the food and equipment, honing the menu to perfection and training themselves for those busy times when we would have to struggle with capacity crowds. The basic food supplies were already in the freezers waiting to be practised on and Marti, though she still couldn't actually come into the Diner, kindly offered to take a load of new samples home to test out on her four children. Aparently they were all judged to be 'fine'.

Then disaster struck in its most familiar and predictable form. I ran out of money. The bank declined to authorise my Maximum Diner credit card, leaving me with only £12.50 cash and some notes earmarked for Ken and André. There was only one way out of the scrape. We would have to open early.

I know. I could have tried borrowing more money and waited to get the Diner completely right first, but that seemed the coward's way. And frankly it seemed daft not to open when customers were popping in every fifteen minutes or so to ask when we would. I was suffused with a Mickey Rooney-esque 'let's put the show on, right here in the barn!' enthusiasm. So, the day after the day after tomorrow it was going to be, no matter if I had to work round the clock to do it.

Two sleepless nights later, I was so tired I could barely stand, let alone hang precariously from a ladder repointing the facade. Forty-eight hours of cleaning and painting were taking their toll. I ate only chocolate and soup (pretty much as I usually do, only smaller portions), and though I tried to snatch the occasional forty winks on the new booth seats, my brain was in such a state of befuddlement that I couldn't tell if I was dreaming or hallucinating. Marti, on the odd moments when she managed to pop in, looked concerned; Ken, for the first time since I'd known him, sounded tetchy; and André sulked, with a pout that stuck out so far I worried he'd topple over. In hindsight it was probably a good decision not to mention that I couldn't pay any wages.

53

The phone rang while I was fast asleep on the floor beside the skirting board I'd been painting. I crawled towards it on hands and knees and it spoke to me, rather oddly, in Spanish. '*Hola Chris, que hay nuevo?* What's up?'

It was Cristina, a Spanish friend I had worked with, and shared a flat with, many years before in Mallorca. These days, she was a flight attendant for Iberia with a complicated love life; one that occasionally necessitated her getting away from Spain for a few days, often staying with me. I was one of her few male friends who could be trusted neither to lecture her about her choice of men nor make a pass at her myself. Or perhaps she just trusted herself not to succumb.

I explained the situation as coherently as I could; the lack of sleep, the lack of money, the need to open very soon, but dozed off mid-sentence. 'Don't worry, Chris. I need to escape from this nightmare of a city for a while. I'm going to come and spend a few days at your place and help you open your diner. I'll get the afternoon flight.' Eight hours later Cristina was perched on a stool in the Diner, slicing *chorizo* and pouring *fino* into tumblers and explaining to me precisely why all Catalan airline pilots are bastards (the married ones especially).

You shouldn't celebrate a friend's ill luck, but having Cristina there was such a boon I might be forgiven. Not only was she the best person I knew to share a kitchen with but she was beautiful too, with dark hair cut short and businesslike, flawless tanned skin and a casual style of dress that gave her the sort of classy look that Jackie Onassis used to aspire to. Cristina's great ambition was to set up her own English-style teashop in Spain, so on her frequent stop-offs at Gatwick I would meet her and we would drive off into the Sussex countryside to try out scones and cakes, and discuss business ideas.

Seeing how exhausted I was, Cristina packed me off home to sleep while she and Ken finished the last of the decorating. I fell immediately into that blissful, empty-headed slumber of someone who has a trusted friend looking after their diner for them.

It lasted just a few hours, though, before I was jolted awake by my mobile phone Muzak. It was Cristina. 'I'm sorry Chris,' she said. 'But it is better if you come now. You have a neighbour here who says he is forbidding you to open.'

It just had to be Tony.

Tony owned the large house next door, a substantial property against which the Diner leant. In the 1960s, Tony and his wife Peg had converted the front of this building into a coffee bar, which became popular with the Mods en route to the seaside on their scooters for a bit of weekend violence. Then in the 1970s they sold the bar to Mr and Mrs Lee, a couple fresh from Hong Kong, who converted it into a Chinese takeaway. Over the years the two families became firm friends and, as little Lees were born, they seemed to fuse together, sharing the properties, with Peggy and Tony acting as surrogate grandparents in a Sussex-Chinese Waltons sort of way.

After retiring as a builder, Tony had become a leading light in the Uckfield Historical and Preservation Society, and he had an encyclopedic knowledge of almost every brick, stone and tile in the town. The Diner, he had told me on our first meeting, was built in the mid-eighteenth century and had seen former use both as an abattoir and a butcher's shop. 'Look', he urged, pointing at the wall, 'you can still see the marks on the old bricks where they sharpened the knives.' Now, given an enthusiastic expert talking about something relevant I can happily listen for hours, drifting into a state of trance-like relaxation. But Tony, alas, rather spoilt the experience with his fussy approach. This was never more apparent than when the subject under historical

55

discussion concerned my right to run a new extractor fan over the roof of my own property.

Due to a Looney Tunes arrangement between solicitors many years ago, I didn't actually own the Diner roof; Peggy and Tony did. So before signing the lease I had to ask them whether they minded my changing the existing extractor pipe that ran across it to a slightly larger one that could cope with the extra fumes from cooking burgers as opposed to lighter bistro-type food. Tony considered the request for some days, talked endlessly about the pros and cons and eventually decided that he might just be able to live with the adjustment. However, while Cristina was busy finishing off the decorating the extractor people arrived and put the pipe up. Tony examined it and discovered with horror that it was a whole inch and a half wider than the last one and that it was stainless steel instead of black. He rushed back indoors and reappeared with a letter, which he solemnly insisted had to be placed in my hands.

The letter read thus:

I, Tony, hereby forbid you, Chris, to put any air through the pipe now sitting on my roof.

It was the planning permission equivalent of a citizen's arrest.

The pipe, Tony argued, was quite possibly a breach of planning laws. But, more crucially, he was anxious about the reaction of the Uckfield Preservation and Historical Society. How would it look if a founder member and leading light was allowing planning infringements to occur on a historic building right beneath his very nose? 'For goodness sake,' he exclaimed, 'I could be drummed out of the Society!'

Extractor systems are always a source of drama. They cost more than almost anything else in the kitchen, cause dreadful problems with neighbours, planners and freeholders, and always go wrong, threatening to asphyxiate first the staff, then the customers. The TV documentaries about Gordon Ramsay and

56

Jamie Oliver opening their own restaurants both featured extractor crises. When it comes to finding 'engineers' to install them, picture the problems one gets with plumbers, then multiply by ten. Extractor engineers are impossible to find, never return your calls, charge whatever they like (and then some), talk gobbledegook about air-flow velocity per second per square inch, fan speeds and 'bend factors', and always, but always, install the system late. Oh, and then you find they've screwed it all up and you're still choking in smoke.

Knowing Tony, I could guess that he had already found a solicitor to put his air-flow banning order on a more legal footing, so simply going next door and trying to bribe or cajole him wasn't an option. I also knew he would need time to get used to the idea, mull over the arguments, consider precedents, etc. I would have to be patient – perhaps modelling myself on Pippin negotiating calmly with Treebeard for reinforcements while the fate of Middle Earth hung in the balance. And I would have to stop Cristina rushing to the back door, shouting at their window and brandishing a waffle iron. One false move could blow it.

At last, though, after several pots of tea and lots of putting the world to rights ('You're not wrong, Tony'), I got him to accept planning permission was inevitable and agree to lift his prohibition. So long as I got the go-ahead of the Preservation Society.

The weekly gathering of the Society was, happily, set for that evening: the time, 6pm; the place, Bridge Cottage, an ancient hall in the centre of town. The rest of the afternoon I spent pacing the Diner, with a tube of mastic in my hand, muttering speeches to the esteemed members of the board, while Cristina, Becky and Ken looked on sympathetically. By 5.30pm the Diner was more or less ready. The menus were written on blackboards, the tiles were all polished, the front window sparkled. We could open, if only Tony would let us.

I went to the meeting with my speech scrawled across the back of a menu. It was a passionate piece of rhetoric that suggested the Diner was a direct descendant of the type of hostelry that Chaucer's pilgrims might have swapped tales in, and how it offered the best, nay almost the only, chance to breathe new life into our historic part of town. As a final flourish (yes, I still have these notes), I was going to conclude that 'if things of inherent importance are to be preserved, then things that have none (like my extractor fan) will need to change'. Hah!

Tony met me outside the hall. He said that he had explained the situation to the members and as a party to the case he would wait outside while I presented my arguments. Then he ushered me towards a large room paved with flagstones and empty except for a large oak table around which the preservationists had convened – all of them, oddly enough, wearing brown. It brought a medieval moot strongly to mind. The chairwoman, a small lady in a beige headscarf, cleared her throat.

'I'm afraid, Mr Nye, that we simply can't understand what your extractor pipe has to do with us.' She looked towards me with a baffled expression. 'Do you think you can enlighten us?'

This was it. I wasn't sure whether to pace about like an attorney in an American courtroom drama, or try and look small and helpless in my chair. The latter seemed the easiest to pull off. 'Tony is worried that the pipe is out of keeping with the look of the building,' I began, 'and that he might be criticised for allowing...' whatever I meant to say next was cut off by a collective exasperated sigh.

'But we don't give a fig about your pipe,' announced the chairwoman to murmured agreement.

'Well, that's great. Thank you very much, er... goodbye,' I replied, earnestly shaking hands with the few people closest to me before turning lightly towards the door. Tony was pacing apprehensively outside. I shook his hand too.

'They don't give a toss about the pipe, Tony,' I said. 'It really is okay.'

'In that case, I will allow you to go ahead,' he replied somewhat stiffly.

'Thanks. Can I have that in writing?'

I returned to the Diner for an opening party organised for family and friends. It was a happy occasion, with gifts and cards and everyone getting drunk, but it was tinged with sadness for me, because I knew that I wouldn't be seeing much of these people any more. I might as well have been sailing to Australia to start a new life, since it is an established fact that opening a restaurant spells the end of the opener's social life. We would be serving the good people of Uckfield seven days a week, from 11am until midnight, and since even I didn't have a clue how it was going to work, it would be a long time before anyone else would be able to run the place for me.

After the party I stayed behind on my own to sort out a few last bits and pieces, and as I sat arranging utensils in the kitchen, a feeling of dread crept over me. It felt like starting at a new school, and suddenly I didn't want to swap the warmth and cosiness of my old friends for the chaos and hassle of a crowded restaurant, each and every day for the foreseeable future. My mood wasn't helped when a bunch of lads appeared at the back door and shouted for a free burger. They were joking, but there was an unmistakable edge of menace.

The next day was opening day. Marti couldn't make it, because she'd had trouble getting a babysitter, but with Cristina's help I got everything ready. The salad items were prepared and put on

59

ice, the burgers put in a neat stack by the griddle, the buns, chips and garlic bread all within easy reach in their allotted places, the cheese and bacon in the fridge, the cooked potatoes ready to make up the hash in a Tupperware container.

At eleven o'clock precisely I turned over the sign on the door and off we went.

The first customer was Ray, the barber from next door, and two of his rugby-playing friends. They seemed impressed by Cristina and huddled round the counter quizzing her on the different ingredients of hash. 'Can you do me the one with the wacky baccy in it?' Ray's friend quipped. I could tell already that the dope jokes were going to pale on me.

Cristina, however, had switched into casual stewardess mode and was handling it all with consummate ease. I wished she were staying but she'd already agreed to work the next day's flight to Palma and, besides, I'd learnt long ago that you can't be too possessive with Cristina.

'Corned Beef Hash, Big Max and Chips and a Maximum Chicken Dinner,' she called out.

The very first order! My mind went blank. Suddenly I didn't know where I was or what I was doing. I hadn't the foggiest idea how to cook anything and would have struggled to make toast, let alone all that lot. Where was I to start?

In moments of total stress, my brain seems to revert to its default setting, which is to get something to eat. So I cut a slice of cheese, got a wedge of tomato, and using a dab of mayonnaise, stuck the two together. Then I added a slice of cucumber to it all, and opened a jar of Branston Pickle that I'd bought just in case. I was well on my way to creating a Scooby-Snack when a dim thought came to me that the Big Max is a burger, so I should put a burger on to cook. Then, a chicken fillet for the Chicken Dinner. Then, the stuff for the hash in a little sauté pan. Slowly my brain clicked into place and I began cooking.

Needless to say I hadn't remembered to open the tin of corned beef in advance and struggled with it, slicing my finger in the process. It didn't matter, though, because now I was in The Zone; frying, griddling, bandaging myself, plating the food and sending it out to Cristina as if I had been doing it for years.

Early the next morning I took Cristina to the airport and said a very fond farewell to her. It was a Friday, not the best day of the week to have as your second day open, with new staff, but I needed the weekend's takings to give to André and Ken on Monday, when they were coming to sort out anything that needed finishing.

Marti arrived early and we sat around self-consciously waiting for the morning's customers. When one did eventually come in I had a mini-crisis again, but gradually it all slotted back into a normal sort of routine. By five o'clock, with about eight hours' work behind me and another eight to go, I was hit by a huge wave of fatigue. Fortunately Catherine had just arrived for her first shift and took over the kitchen. She had been working in a teashop all her teenage life, so she rearranged things to her satisfaction and then concentrated on looking after the orders while I fell asleep on the floor of the storeroom for a few minutes.

We served a slow but steady stream of customers. most of whom made appreciative noises about the food. It was all quite relaxing. Then at 11.15pm the proverbial shit and fan made contact as a stampede of drunks arrived from the pub, ushered in by Marti and Becky. 'Bottle of Stella and a cheeseburger, mate,' was the order over and over and over again as a mob four-deep crowded the counter. Some people wanted two bottles of beer, and amid the hubbub and while cooking about fifty burgers I had to try and explain the licensing laws to my new customers.

Those laws, as far as I understand them, state that you can serve alcohol until midnight so long as it's drunk on the premises and so long as the alcohol is ancillary to the meal. In other words,

61

your customer has to have arrived for a meal and then thought, 'You know what, I think I'll have a beer as well!' rather than 'Right, time for beer. Oh, and I'll have a burger.' That's quite a concept to get through to a very drunk person at 11.30 at night. And it was made worse by the fact that I'd told Becky, rather stupidly, the little-known fact that restaurants can sell alcohol to sixteen-year-olds so long as they're eating a meal. Becky had made sure that everyone in town knew this fact, so we had a good percentage of Uckfield's thirteen-year-olds in, with the boys all trying to look tall and serious, putting on daft, theatrically deep voices as they ordered beer.

Despite a few awkward exchanges, I managed to avoid getting lynched. In fact, I seemed to be everyone's new best friend. By a quarter past twelve, everyone had been served and was either sitting on the steps outside, or swinging on Tony's gate. I took a quick glance inside the till and it was full. I rang my brother and woke him up to say that his investment was safe.

How precipitous was that!

The Three Garys

A PATTERN OF TRADE SOON EMERGED, with Friday and Saturday nights providing most of the stress and takings, other evening trade rolling along okay, but daytime pickings distinctly thin. A few local office or shop workers might come in for lunch, or a group of kids might drop by for a milkshake after school, but for much of the day it was worryingly quiet. Some mornings I'd only have one customer, an elderly, almost blind, evangelical Christian called Miss Green, who would sit for hours over a cup of tea, with maybe a slice of bread on the side (margarine pre-ferred), enthusing loudly about God. The gist of it was that God had been wonderful to her and had arranged for her the most glorious life – except, perhaps, for the blindness and the hospi-talisations following fractures and cuts. On some mornings, as a concession to my sounding a bit hung over she would tone down the cheerful stoicism a bit and ask how the Diner was getting on, or relay nuggets of news from her vigil with the radio.

63

I liked Miss Green. She was one of those doughty, companionable sorts who does wonders for moral fibre. There were moments, however, when I would watch her shuffling towards the Diner, arms outstretched, bag wrapped around her chest like a parachute, and wonder about the customer profile I'd so hopefully drawn up. When planning my venture, I'd imagined the place thronged with hip, youthful types, sipping cappuccinos and greeting new friends who'd rushed to the new diner to be part of the in-crowd. Still, it was early days, and compared with some of my post-pub regulars, such as Guppy and The Three Garys, Miss Green was a model customer.

I first met Guppy when he fell through the door in a drunken haze one night just before closing time and landed in a heap on the floor. It was obvious from the word go that he was trouble. Or, more precisely, it was obvious from the word 'c-u-n-t' tattooed across his knuckles, as he gripped the counter and attempted to pull himself to his feet. I heard a sharp intake of breath from behind me and turned to catch a glimpse of Becky crossing herself.

'I'll have... hang on,' he paused, preparing himself before attempting the multi-task of thinking while standing up, 'chips... and a beer.'

'Sorry, we're just closing,' I said as nonchalantly as I could, while signalling to Becky to nip behind him and put the 'Closed' sign up on the door.

'Alright, just the beer.'

'We're not allowed to serve alcohol now, we're closed,' I replied amiably, indicating the still-swinging 'Closed' sign.

'No beer?'

'Sorry, no. No beer.'

Guppy seemed to sober up a little. He leant over the counter, allowing me a close-up of the home-made tattoos that covered his face, and breathed fumes straight up my nose that spoke of alcohol, cigarettes, methadone and prison.

'Give me a beer or I'll nut the fuck out of you, twat.'

Well, there's a time to stand up and be counted, but this wasn't it. 'Large chips was it, mate?' I said cheerily.

He paused again, then: 'Yeah, with chilli sauce.'

Now, did you notice what I did there? By cleverly ignoring the issue of the beer, I diverted Guppy to less contentious matters. It's a time-honoured technique: when things get sticky you revert to the other side's previous proposal, and ignore all the nastiness that's built up since. It helped the Kennedy brothers avoid nuclear war during the Cuban Missile Crisis in 1963, and it helped me now, as Guppy waited quite happily for his chips while perhaps, through the alcoholic haze, wondering whether or not he'd been tricked.

Fortunately, he never got to the end of that contemplation, for just then, belying the old cliché about there never being one around when you need them, two policemen walked in. They knew Guppy.

'Hello, mate! Out again, then?' said the younger one, as he led Guppy quietly off to the car for a lift home. His senior colleague meanwhile took me to one side and said they were concerned down at the station at 'the element the Diner was attracting'. The general feeling was that we had been misguided in writing on the back of the menu, 'We're open 'til midnight, so you can come in when you're rat-arsed.'

Frankly, the joke had started to wear a bit thin anyway. While most of the drunken youths (in Uckfield the term extends from nine to thirty) weren't threatening the staff or me directly, they were looking for post-pub entertainment and if they couldn't generate it amongst themselves they were more than happy to

65

see who else they might provoke. So it was like *Straw Dogs* every Friday night as the alpha types tried to impress their giggling underlings. At ordering time (11.20pm), the sheer volume of people demanding food kept trouble to a minimum, as the entire drinking population of Uckfield crammed against the counter with their fivers waving, yelling at Catherine and me (Marti hadn't been able to do evening shifts, after all). But when the food had all been served, the wrappers chucked on the floor, and people were replete (11.30pm), the effects of nine pints of lager would kick in and the trouble would start.

Firstly there was the stealing. At 10.30 each night we removed those items that might be used as missiles, such as ashtrays, ketchups, salts and peppers. But then pictures started going missing, and pot plants, magazine racks, even mops and brooms. So everything had to be taken out and stored, leaving just tables and chairs. To be fair, what was stolen usually came back, either thrown through the back door (which was left open to cool whoever was doing the cooking), or returned from nearby gardens by the few neighbours who were still speaking to me. The lane at the side of the Diner looked over the back of the kitchen, so on particularly fierce nights we were surrounded, and it was all a bit too much like Rorke's Drift.

Then there were the food fights, which we dealt with by reducing the portion sizes to a level whereby every chip was precious. Over zealous shaking of ketchup bottles caused two serious incidents that had to be broken up by the police, and there was once a running battle up the High Street after one Friday night yob had put vinegar on another's chips. We introduced sachets, and I also took the advice of the police and stopped serving alcohol after 11pm.

As we all now know, it's legal to serve drinks to anyone over the age of sixteen, up to midnight, even without an adult present, so long as they're sitting down for a meal. But it's a less known fact that it is illegal to serve alcohol to anyone who is drunk. Rather sensible licensing laws, in theory. In practice, of course, it didn't make a spot of difference, because people just bought a couple of bottles on the way out from the pub and drank them at the Diner. (I was supposed to confiscate them?)

We still let one person have lager after 11pm. He was the owner of the local building firm and a man so dangerous and fearsome I shall only call him 'Fat Harry'. In fact, no, I shall just call him 'Harry'. Harry sat at the end of the counter on his special stool, gazing at Becky, and occasionally pointing out when one or other of the yobs was 'bang out of order'. No one quibbled.

I saw it as a kind of cheap protection scheme. Employing bouncers was not an option, as we would have needed half a dozen big ones, just to sell a few burgers. And if I'd employed a cut-price, weedy bouncer I could see myself having to wade in and help, and there was a strict 'no fisticuffs' clause written into my personal contract.

There were three main troublemakers, and weirdly they were all called Gary.

Gary A was a mechanic and some kind of lieutenant to Harry. His brief was to stand on the sidelines quietly egging his numb-skull sub-yobs into violence with, for example, a quiet 'Eh Robbo, that bloke in the tie just called you a wanker' in Robbo's ear. Afterwards, as the bloke in the tie lay groaning on the floor, Gary would help him to his feet and say, 'Blimey mate, that Robbo's a mentalist isn't he? Nutter!' Though Gary A had been implicated as a ringleader in the nationally reported 'Crowborough–Uckfield riots' I never felt especially worried about him, sensing that his desire for quality late-night burgers would keep him sweet enough.

The same couldn't be said when it came to Gary B. He was truly nasty, with a face covered in scars and pockmarks, and a prison stretch for beating up a policewoman. From Monday to Friday he was a scaffolder but at weekends Gary B led a subset of Uckfield lowlife who had taken all the cheeky-chappy charm out of being a hooligan and replaced it with more violence. Gary B had adopted a kind of cartoon nastiness that involved looking at you with half-closed eyes, head lolling like he was permanently stoned, talking in that voice that Kenny Everett used to employ for Sid Snot. The first time he came in I found the whole act so laughable that I treated him like he was meant to be funny. Big mistake. I had to be rescued by Becky when things got a bit too *GoodFellas*.

Last of the fearsome threesome was Gary C, one of the bored youths who had been hanging around the Diner waiting for us to open. He wasn't so much fearsome as intensely annoying, in the ways that fourteen-year-old boys specialise in. His gang was comprised not only of the neglected teens and tweens who you expect to see loitering around the off-licences, but also the rich kids that like to hang around with them. Perhaps the latter provide the cash and the former provide the street cred and ideas. Then together they create mayhem.

The main bone of contention I had with them was over smoking. Though I allowed smoking in the Diner, I didn't want it filled up with fourteen-year-olds puffing away while sharing a Diet Coke, which is precisely what they wanted to do. They would roam around each non-school night, in a gang of up to thirty, ages ranging from twelve to sixteen, most of them drunk, all smoking. At some point they would invade the Diner.

Not all at once, though, they were smarter than that. A couple of teenagers would come in for chips and milkshakes, which seemed nice. We'd chat and get a bit of rapport going and everyone would relax. Then some girls would come past, see their mate with a new boyfriend and come in to check him out. They'd invariably have a few boys in tow, including Gary C, who would sit at a different table, trying to look cool while filling up the ashtray and not buying anything. With three of the six tables occupied for about £4.75, I would intervene and tell the crew that if they weren't going to buy anything they'd have to leave. At which point Gary C would seize his chance and say that no other customers were coming in anyway, so why didn't I just chill. 'I'll chill when I bloody well feel like it,' was the irresistible reply – and always a mistake, because he'd then tut and say there was no need for 'fucking language' (to titters from the crowd), but alright, he'd have a Coke if it would make me happy. So now I'd have seven kids filling my restaurant on a Friday night, for a total profit of £1.25, sipping from bottles of vodka concealed in their Puffa jackets and looking at me smugly. At which point I'd start getting cross.

Eventually push would come to shove, literally, and I would have to physically throw 'C' out onto the pavement, his mates would follow, and then I'd have to patrol outside so nobody could chuck a bottle through the window. All this was awkward enough, but if there was a 'normal' family trying to enjoy a meal at the same time it was embarrassing beyond belief. One minute I would be taking their order, all suave and in control and the next I'd be chasing youths up the High Street before coming back breathless, surreptitiously trying to wipe the sweat off my face as I served their drinks and apologised for the 'minor little interruption'.

I'd hate to sound here like some sort of whining shopkeeper moaning on about yob culture because I'm not at all sure that yob culture exists. What I've discovered is that yobs, once they're 'off-duty,' can often be the very brightest and nicest of our youth. The drunk vomiting in Leicester Square might be the son of our Prime Minister, the kid selling dope to his mates might be the Foreign Secretary's, while the couple shagging in the alleyway might well be your Employees of the Month. Even among our post-pub crowd there were a few who managed to stay perfectly pleasant. Dani and Scott, for instance, were a lovely couple who would always be returning glasses and plates and thanking me above the hubbub for a great burger or asking Catherine how her old man was doing. And some of the drunken banter was quite funny. Sure, I didn't want to be serving a great crowd of them food at 11.30 every night but my problem wasn't so much with yobs, per se. My problem was with the violent psychopaths that hid out among them.

I thought of closing early at weekends, of course, but we weren't making enough money the rest of the week to dispense with the vital post-pub trade. So there I was standing up for the amusement of the Garys and their mates like an inept supply teacher, wondering if I could run a business and stay out of Casualty at the same time.

In more reflective moments, I mused on how the problem wouldn't arise if we could attract a classier clientele. The dream for the new restaurateur in these celebrity-obsessed days is to get one in your establishment, so I had made a list of potential stars who might drop by: Paul McCartney lives in Sussex, Bob Hoskins lives somewhere off the A22, a Spice Girl (I forget which) was spotted in nearby Lewes, and Jane Torvill has been seen in Tesco's. Sky Sports presenter and ex-gymnast Suzanne Dando actually grew up in Uckfield and occasionally came home to see her mum, bringing her ex-*Neighbours* actor hus-band. I looked forward to signed photos (*Chris, mate – Your veggieburgers Please Please Me! – Macca xx*) gracing the walls of the Diner before very long.

Imagine my delight, then, when Jilly Goolden turned up one Friday evening. Jilly Goolden? Presenter of BBC2's *Food and Drink*, regular on *Call My Bluff*? It was a start anyway, and once Becky and Catherine heard the magic words 'She's on TV,' they leapt into action. Was the cutlery buffed to its finest stainless steeliest? Did Jilly have the very fullest, whitest salt pot on the table? Had any youth amusingly loosened the top of the ketchup bottle so that when she shook it, it would go all over the person behind her? Was the music just right for a person of Jilly's age and social standing? Was my apron clean enough, but not too clean, obviously? Should I speak to her? How was my hair?

Jilly was exactly the kind of contact I needed to get into television. Keith Floyd, after all, was discovered by some hungry TV executive when he was running a restaurant in Bristol, and offered his own show just like that. Thoughts of my own cookery show flashed across my mind: *Christopher's Complete Cookery Course: Series One, Chips to Hash*. Meanwhile, everything that was to pass Jilly's lips had to be checked and rechecked, while I sent Becky out to the off-licence for their top wine. In the event Jilly chose Budweiser (she was disappointed it wasn't the Czech version – that's our Jilly!) and a Veggie Farmhouse Hash with Side Salad and Blue Cheese Dressing. I'm glad to say she ate most of it.

While Jilly and 'her party' (as we say) were finishing their meal and were reported to be relaxed and happy, I was agonising about whether or not to say hello and introduce myself, or treat her like any other customer. Eventually, after a frantic whispered discussion with Becky and Catherine that Jilly probably heard, I decided to compromise, and say a bright and breezy 'Hello' – but not, crucially, 'Hello, Jilly.' The important thing, we all agreed, was not to jump in with both feet and ask for a guest spot on *Food and Drink* straightaway, but first to wow her with my easy manner and crisp, calm sense of catering know-how.

I approached the table and managed a friendly but slightly too high-pitched, panicky almost, 'Everyone finished?' I told myself to calm down and started clearing the plates, before suddenly blurting out 'HELLO!' much too loudly, completely out of context, and to no one in particular, then following it up by emitting a sound that was part sigh, part ingested scream. Jilly, Jilly's husband, Jilly's children, Jilly's friends, Jilly's friends' children, all looked at me in surprise before one of the kids offered a tentative 'Hello?' back, in a small voice.

After that I left Becky to sort out the puddings and retreated to the sink, where I furiously did the dishes and cursed my lack of sophistication. 'For God's sake, man,' I told myself. 'Paul McCartney will probably be in next week with his lot, maybe Ringo, too. How will you cope with that!' I shouldn't, however, have been torturing myself about these events, for there were more immediate ones at hand. Had I looked at the clock I would have noticed that it had just gone eleven.

Jilly and the Gooldens had evidently enjoyed themselves so much that they had lingered almost half an hour over coffee and ice cream. This was a problem. Time was ticking on and we still hadn't cleared away the movable items in the restaurant on the grounds that Jilly might think it odd if we leant over her to take a picture down or removed the chair that her daughter was sitting on. I was still muttering to myself over the dishes when Becky appeared ashen-faced at the door. 'For Chrissake, it's ten past eleven', she hissed. 'What are we going to do?'

The enormity of the problem suddenly hit me. Within minutes our very first celeb was about to share her dining space with Sussex's dimmest lager-boys. I hurriedly wrote out the bill and lunged through the door, determined to bundle her out under any pretext – we were closed, we were on fire – but was just seconds too late. 'OY! ISS THAT WOMAN OFF THE TELLY!', came the unmistakably slurred voice of Gary C. Becky, Catherine and

I quickly formed a human cordon to cover the exit path for Jilly, while she and her party gathered up their coats. Fortunately they had already mentally left so they didn't seem to notice the drunken comments as a few more regulars stumbled in; and they were already well round the corner at 11.20pm when the rest of the youth of Uckfield swept in like a mighty Atlantic roller crashing onto the beach and the cry went up: 'Bottle of Stella and a cheeseburger, mate.'

As we went onto autopilot and concentrated on cooking and serving as quickly as possible, it became evident that the necessary preparation hadn't been done. Whereas the operation was normally slick as a pit stop at Silverstone, tonight we kept running out of things that we'd forgotten to take out of the freezers ('What do you mean you've got no fucking burgers?'), and the fryer went cold because in the excitement over Jilly I had forgotten to boost the power on it. Bored youths having to wait ages for food quickly saw their chance for mischief. While I was rushing around the kitchen like a helium-injected version of *Ready, Steady, Cook!*, listening to snatches of Catherine and Becky's postmortem of our star-studded night, the place erupted in scuffles, shouts and laughter.

It couldn't go on. I had to abandon the cooking and investigate. Pushing my way through the crowd I discovered Robbo trying drunkenly to bundle my expensive American swing bin through the door. I grappled it back and turned to place it by the wall when I noticed something else had gone. Oh, yes. The television was missing. And so were some of the seats. The crowd went quiet, expectant, and a small clearing formed around me. I expect there are more intimidating sights than violent hooligans out for trouble – for example, I've always found the sight of a

73

very thin woman playing the cello particularly alarming – but this must have been what the early Christians felt like in a little provincial amphitheatre trying to negotiate with the lions.

'What happened to the TV, then?' I asked the mob, in as calm a voice as I could manage.

Drunken lads stifled giggles.

'What TV would that be then, Chris?' said Gary C.

'The TV that until a few minutes ago was on the wall over there.'

More muffled guffaws.

'I hope you're not calling us thieves…?' menaced Robbo, to murmured agreement from the crowd. Since I'd just caught him nicking a designer trashcan, I felt the evidence was on my side, but you can't reason with these people, and as I turned to go back to the kitchen a tomato ketchup bottle flew over my head and smashed on the wall, spattering it bright red, just as the police arrived.

Catherine was able to identify the ketchup thrower and the police escorted him to their car, where he immediately burst into tears. His life would be ruined, he cried, if they arrested him. He'd just got a job as a social security clerk and he'd be bound to lose it. Some hooligan. In the end we relented and the police let him off with a caution.

I returned to the (now empty) Diner and began to help Catherine and Becky clear up the mess. Something else was missing apart from the few chairs. Ah yes, that nice picture that had recently been hanging above Jilly's head.

Good, as we know, can sometimes come out of bad and though we never did get the TV, light fittings or pictures back I discovered a whole new respect for Becky and Catherine. Catherine especially, whose dad was a builder, and who had grown up knowing some of the toughest site hands in Uckfield, showed an impressive confidence in dealing with the yobs and the police. She seemed, in fact, to be taking on the role I had imagined for Marti – the mature organiser who works overtime when needed and calmly defuses the trickiest situations. Marti might also have been good at these things. But then I never got a chance to judge, as Marti was almost entirely absent.

Ironically, Marti was one of those caring types who like to 'be there' for people. When teenage friends of her four children were kicked out of their homes, Marti was there for them; when they needed someone to go with them to the police station, or to the doctor's or the dole, Marti was there too. Even at work (and Marti only managed nineteen out of thirty shifts) she'd be there for someone, so long as they didn't actually want to order some food. Ten minutes into the shift some sullen teenager would inevitably appear and Marti would light a fag and prepare for a mammoth counselling session.

Having Mother Earth on your books just isn't all it's cracked up to be. A push came to a shove when Marti bought a guard dog and then had to stay at home to protect the kids and babysitter from being bitten. We had words and Marti opted to leave with a month's wages and promised to come and do shifts whenever we were stuck. It was the last I saw of her.

At college I remember one of the business lectures dwelling on a rather alarming statistic: that to calculate the cost of replacing a trained and experienced employee, you multiply their hourly wage by three hundred. So just taking the minimum wage of £4.10 per hour, it will cost the employer £1230 to replace his or her staff. A lot of people will dismiss this as a load of crap, just as I had. But they shouldn't. There are the obvious costs, like advertising the post, taking time off for interviewing, induction, training and so on, and then there are the less predictable ones –

75

little leakages of productivity here and there, the demoralising effects of staff losing colleagues. When everything is included I think £1230 could seem like a bargain.

So when it came to replacing Marti I was determined to get it absolutely right.

Darren seemed the perfect candidate. He'd had experience in the trade, came with good references, an ability to turn his hand to anything from car maintenance to origami with napkins to breaking up yob fights. He had that intensity of ambition that not going to college can give – and at nineteen he was engaged and managing a mortgage. I didn't know it was legal to take on that much responsibility at that age.

The only problem was that Becky and Catherine took against him from the moment he arrived.

To be fair, Darren was a curious chap. Ginger hair, nothing wrong with that, unless it's combined with little round eyes in a great white slab of a face that reminded me of Wensleydale cheese. He tended to stoop slightly, too, and as he beetled about getting things done, he resembled just slightly a large ape with a clipboard. Darren really was a treasure.

I should add that he was also an ideas man. Darren's ideas were ceaseless, and one of the first was that we should be offering kids' birthday parties, what with Uckfield having so many kids. 'Great idea, Darren. Good to have some positive input,' I replied. But it wasn't. Holding birthday parties at the Diner was a very, very bad idea indeed.

Make a Wish

THE POINT ABOUT BIRTHDAY PARTIES is that they don't need to make much money – indeed don't need to make any money at all. Their purpose is to tap into the mysterious force of kids, known in the trade as 'pester power'. The theory is that children who attend a party will have such a great time that they will drag their own families in, and they in turn will become regular customers, tell their friends, etc, etc. From the restaurant point of view, it can all be done as a loss leader, with the food and drink taken off the already cheap children's menu, and a free party bag for each kid, with party poppers, streamers and all manner of noisy treats thrown in, not to mention a member of staff to look after the children, and a cake at cost price.

Looking back I can see this was marketing largesse bordering on desperation. Although an immediate hit amongst mothers and fathers, its cash-flow benefits were slow to show and, more importantly, the staff hated the whole business. Neither Darren nor I had any idea what sort of noise children can make once you dose them up with Coke and give them a whistle to whistle and poppers to pop. Before long they'd be tearing round the Diner like a troop of overactive gibbons, climbing all over the furniture, dropping food down the back of the seats, yanking pictures off the walls and smudging the beautifully drawn blackboards... and that's just while booking the venue.

I liked the idea that the Maximum Diner was the kind of unstuffy place where people could relax and not be embarrassed about their kids' behaviour; after all, children are meant to be noisy and mischievous. But at the same time, there were these moments when it would have been nice if they could just...

KEEP THEIR BLOODY KIDS UNDER CONTROL.

FOR CHRISSAKES, CAN'T THEY?

JUST ONCE.

JESUS!

The worst thing was that most mothers didn't really want their parties on quiet weekdays. They wanted them on Sunday afternoons and, though I tried to stop them, I'm a sucker for a pleading mother and I usually ended up agreeing. My reluctance was because there were other forces at work on Sundays. It seems amazing now, but only a few short years ago pubs had to close their doors at three o'clock on a Sunday afternoon, and not open again until seven. That left four hours for the drinking population of Uckfield to fill, and everyone knew that we had an all-day restaurant liquor licence.

On top of this, some of the more sober members of the Sussex population go out 'motoring' in the countryside on Sundays, often with an elderly relative, and like to stop somewhere for tea along the way, which in Uckfield meant us because we were the only place open. So they would stand outside, 'nice' couples wearing car coats and some kind of hat, peer in suspiciously and eventually come in, standing awkwardly by the door waiting to be seated. They'd ask if we did cream teas, but usually settle for a toasted sandwich while asking for the music to be turned down. I liked these people (indeed I rather harboured an ambition to be one myself one day) and felt protective towards them.

It was inevitable, however, that all of these three forces – small children out to party, Uckfield's drunken underclass, and middle-aged motorists – would one day come together in the 300 square foot of the Maximum Diner, in a kind of 'Perfect Storm'. And it happened one Sunday afternoon in March – unfortunately on Darren's day off.

It all began so calmly. I had decorated the tables in streamers, balloons and party poppers, and a cake was ready in the back room with seven candles on it. Becky was coming in to serve the children, and since the party was organised for a quarter to three, I hoped the sight of a full restaurant would keep the yobs out when they turned up in the pub interval. Meanwhile an elderly couple from nearby Tunbridge Wells had arrived and were scanning the menu for tea and scones.

A dozen or so eager young faces appeared at the window and charged in, ripping up the streamers and punching the balloons about like the 'knee-high nihilists' that Attila the Stockbroker once described in his poem, 'A Bang and a Wimpy'. One child was so overcome with excitement she started crying before she'd even sat down, and I felt like joining her since Becky hadn't yet turned up. While Birthday-Boy-Mum was trying to comfort crying-girl, Birthday-Boy-Dad, a well-spoken sort dressed in jeans and sports jacket in the Jeremy Clarkson mould, did a remarkably ineffectual job of keeping control of the other kids.

With Becky now evidently not coming, I had the same feeling I used to get as a child when I was falling off my bike but hadn't

hit the ground yet, the split second of quiet misery as you con-
template imminent suffering. Time to delegate. I got Birthday-
Boy-Dad to take the children's order while I got Mr and Mrs
Tunbridge Wells served.

Silly mistake. Had the mother taken the order it would have
been a can of drink each with a straw in the top, instead of which
the kids were testing Dad's order-taking abilities with as complicated a set of milkshake flavour combos as possible. I wondered
whether I should point out that a strawberry-raspberry-lime-
toffee milkshake isn't necessarily going to be nice... but what the
hell, it wasn't my car they were going to be sick in on the way
home. During the delay while I set to work on the shakes,
Birthday-Boy-Dad got the kids to wash their hands, prompting
a water fight in the toilet. But, with no sign of relief from Becky,
I was becoming resigned to letting the little chaps cause as much
mayhem as they liked.

Birthday-Boy-Mum tried to restore order but it was too late for
reason, and as she loudly cursed her 'useless' husband the children ran back into the restaurant yelling as loudly as they could
and spraying water droplets from their sodden hair. Meanwhile,
Mr Tunbridge Wells's mouth was now set in a firm line as he irritably fended off balloons floating in his direction. But he and his
wife were stuck waiting for their toasted sandwiches to appear,
and it takes more than a children's riot to make the British walk
out on a food order.

80   Time to put on loud music! As the Spice Girls sang out
'Wannabe' the children zigazigared along and the food was coming on nicely. Then I turned to see Guppy looking through the
window. He saw the children, smiled excitedly and came staggering in. The kids saw a funny swaying man with drawings on
his face and assumed the clown had arrived; a great cheer went
up. Birthday-Boy-Dad saw his worst nightmare approaching
and whispered to me, 'Watch out for the situation, will you, it

could get sticky.' The Tunbridge Wellses stared into their teacups and tried to look inconspicuous. Birthday-Boy-Mum and I looked at each other; so *that* was why I hadn't wanted her to come on Sunday.

Guppy, encouraged by the children's positive reaction, picked up a balloon and bounced it on his nose like a performing seal. 'Come on kids, catch the ball!' he cried. Soon all the children were leaping about playing catch with one of the most violent and disturbed men in the Weald. The noise was enormous but it was friendly and the tension dropped, as it seemed that perhaps we were going to get away with it after all. I put the food on the table and the children sat down to eat.

Guppy retired to the last empty table, saying a cheery 'Hello, mate' to the couple from Tunbridge Wells, and occasionally singing a little 'zigazig', long after the Spice Girls had moved on to another song. Birthday-Boy-Dad seized his chance to regain some credibility and went and perched on the end of Guppy's table, chatting about which of the kids was likely to be the next prop forward for England. I don't think Guppy knew what a prop forward was (some kind of scaffolding pole, perhaps?), but he played along commendably.

Then Guppy's mates turned up, having been delayed at the off-licence buying enough beer to get them through a four-hour dry spell. There were five of them, including Guppy's girlfriend, I assume, since they launched into an extended snog. I recognised her as someone I had interviewed for a job. 'Such a nice person', I'd thought at the time, and would have employed her if Catherine hadn't used a very strong veto. I hoped she wouldn't hold rejection against me.

The Guppy party, however, seemed in good humour. Birthday-Boy-Dad scarpered back to his wife's table and, since the Guppy group couldn't all sit together, two of them went and joined the Tunbridge Wellses, keeping in touch with their mates at the far

81

end of the restaurant by shouting things like, 'Show us yer tits and I'll buy you a burger' and 'Piss off, she hasn't got any tits. They're only worth a couple of chips.'

I tried ramping the music up but this made the Guppy party shout louder. I hoped the noise of the kids might drown them out, but they had gone mysteriously quiet, and the one who had been crying earlier was starting to look quivery again. Birthday-Boy-Dad and I looked at each other, clearly hoping the other would ask them to tone it down.

I sighed, resigned to the fact that it was my job, and approached the table. However, before I got there, a shrill, firm voice piped up. 'Will you please moderate your language? There are little ears listening.' It was Mrs Tunbridge Wells.

'Little ears'? The two youths sharing her table, dead ringers for the kid in those 'I can handle it' anti-heroin adverts from the 1980s, meekly shut up, and quietly gave me their orders amid an awkward silence.

Guppy alone seemed oblivious to the strained atmosphere and blathered on regardless about how much he loved children and why didn't he and his girlfriend have a go at getting pregnant, while my other twenty-one customers sat in an agony of tension, wondering whether he meant right now in the Diner and, if so, what the lady in the tweed skirt and sensible shoes was going to do about it. Mum tried to jolly the children up, but it once more looked like the party was heading for disaster. You could have cut the atmosphere with a knife.

Which reminded me to get the birthday cake.

In the back room I grimly lit the seven candles on the cake which I'd spent most of the previous evening icing, muttering 'I will NOT do this again' with each candle. But as I brought the cake into the room, with the lights down and the candles lit, everyone went 'Aaaarrrhh,' and launched into a lusty rendition of 'Happy Birthday' – Guppy, his girlfriend, their mates, tweedy

Tunbridge Wellses, Birthday-Boy-Mum with tears in her eyes, Birthday-Boy-Dad in a warbly baritone. It was a special moment.

Half an hour later, as parents collected little ones, and a beaming Birthday-Boy smiled up at me as he collected his lollipop, Becky arrived at the door, full of mouthed apologies for being late. There was an awkward shuffling round of people as yob went and sat with yob and churchgoer settled down with churchgoer, but eventually everyone was sorted out. Birthday-Boy-Mum asked if we could arrange another party for her nephew the next month.

I hesitated a moment to consider this. It had been quite touching, with a definite sense of community spirit about the endeavour. But then I thought of Guppy.

'No sorry, we've got some health and safety issues we need to resolve,' I replied, and went back to sweeping up the mountain of debris left on the floor.

The Art of War

I WOULDN'T WANT TO GIVE THE IMPRESSION that our customers in those first few months of opening were solely gangs of violent drunks or rampaging tweenies. After all, we still had Miss Green, and there were other perfectly unassuming, well-behaved regulars who would pop in now and again, eat food without tossing it at each other, and even leave tips.

This kind of clientele could create an air of quiet optimism about the place – at least, when we were reasonably full – and I began to look forward to seeing some of the regulars. One woman, in particular, always lifted my spirits – a friendly, good-looking mother, mid-thirties, with bright blonde hair, who would come in with her two angelic toddlers and delightedly sample new parts of the menu. While her children danced around to whatever music I was playing, or poked their little smiling faces into the kitchen, she would chat with me about cooking and the general ups and downs of catering life.

Sometimes she'd even bring friends along, proudly showing off the Diner to them and asking me how it was all going.

Then the rotten cow opened her own café bar. It was further down the High Street, financed in partnership with the very friends that she'd been so pleased to introduce me to, and it was called The Oasis. There was a swish bar downstairs with tables spiling out onto the pavement and a restaurant upstairs, over-looking the Uck. The menu was similar to mine, albeit with a slightly more Italian-American feel, and it not only pulled busi-ness away from the Diner during the day, but right from the out-set it started to cut into our post-pub trade – as it, too, had a restaurant licence.

Fortunately this very success proved its undoing. Within weeks of opening, The Oasis had an even worse yob problem than us, and her dream of offering a sophisticated open-air bar was trampled by crowds of thirteen- and fourteen-year-olds hanging around waiting to be passed bottles of beer by their older sib-lings. A front page headline in the local paper had the Mayor describing the restaurant as 'a drinking man's hell' (whatever that is), and it closed down soon after.

One competitor had been seen off, but elsewhere the word seemed to have got out that Uckfield was the place to open. The competition was about to get hotter. Over the next six months a Little Chef opened on the bypass. A fish and chip shop opened in upper Uckfield, then an Indian restaurant, then a Chinese takeaway. Toppers, the local pizza takeaway, moved out of its premises by the bus station at the bottom of town and into a pub directly across the road from us, which they turned into a 'pizza pub' – sort of a gastro-pub run by people who can't cook. This struck me as rather a neat, alliterative synergy, but they spoilt it by announcing that fondue would be a speciality. So it would be a 'pizza and fondue pub' – such a crazy idea that I feared it might actually work. Darren and I went off to check it out one evening

85

but, alas, the prongs hadn't arrived from Switzerland, so we were disappointed.

Meanwhile, and potentially more serious, Toppers had sold their old premises to a large man with a beard who looked like Hagrid's scruffier cousin. He opened a burger takeaway, much cheaper than mine and in a better position. And he called it Burger Off. Excellent choice!

As each competitor opened, we launched into a pre-emptive campaign against them – a tactic taught to me while working as bar manager at a themed restaurant-bar in Cambridge that served Tex Mex food and took the American South as its theme. Then one of the big breweries started a rival chain (let's call it Old South), opening a branch near us and headhunting many of our staff. Their menu was the same old stuff as the rest of us, and the decor featured some rather lame 'WALK/DON'T WALK' signs and American car number plates, but it became popular with the less discerning people of Cambridge. Eventually our area manager noticed the dented sales figures and demanded to know what we were doing by means of counter attack. Seeing our blank looks, he sighed heavily and told us what we should have done.

Firstly, we should have known Old South was coming well before they started stealing our staff, from checking each month the planning applications lodged at the local council offices. If a vigorous campaign to deny them planning failed, we should have schmoozed our best staff, if necessary giving them post-shift foot massages and free vodka, until they loved us like babies. Then we should have visited other restaurants in the Old South chain to discover exactly how they looked and what they sold, and taken a few of their Unique Selling Points and copied them. For example, if Old South's speciality was some kind of Southern Pie thing, and they had red-checked tablecloths, we should have introduced our own Special Southern Pie and used red-checked tablecloths in the weeks before they opened, so when Old South opened they would have looked like a pale imitation of us. Additionally, we should have leafleted all around their premises and bombarded our own customers with money-off vouchers.

This is the technique known as 'falling on your adversary like a thunderbolt' as proposed in Sun Tsu's *The Art of War*, a strategy manual written in China around 500BC which is still followed by presidents, military commanders, captains of industry and sports stars who want to gain an upper hand against competitors. Our area manager at the time was steeped in the book, and swore blind that its principles held good for the modern catering trade, but I kept finding myself nodding off mid-paragraph. Sure, it felt good buying it, and flicking through it ostentatiously on the train. But it's soooooo boring, and I think questions do have to be asked of its relevance today. For example, 'when woods move, this indicates an enemy's clandestine approach'. Well, yes, I suppose it might.

Nonetheless, I like to think that our tactics at the Diner would have got a murmur of approval from Mr Tsu. While keeping a sharp eye out for moving shrubbery, we decided to take on the Little Chef at its own game and compete with them for a slice of the breakfast market. We added a whole range of artery-busting American-style breakfast choices to the menu and gave them names that should have become at least as famous as Little Chef's 'Early Starter' – 'The 3 Egg Superpower', a high-protein breakfast for 'energetic weekenders', and the 'Big Plate Special', a breakfast served on a Special Big Plate. Then we helpfully marked the menu with the enormous prices Little Chef were charging for the same meal and, once the meals were established,

87

branched out with healthier, low-fat alternatives. The service was an immediate hit, especially with new couples, and if their warm body language and generally sleep-deprived appearance was anything to go by we seemed to become just the place to enjoy a post-shag pick-you-up. I would have liked to have advertised this service in the paper, but somehow I just couldn't get the wording right.

Breakfast trade became a modest success. But unfortunately it didn't have the desired knock-on effect for the rest of the shifts. In fact, for large chunks of the day we continued to be almost empty, with no one but Miss Green to chat to – if you discount a series of salespeople. Shopkeepers idling away in empty shops are easy prey for salespeople and my afternoons were punctuated by discussions with persuasive men and women trying to sell me cheap electricity, tea towels, raffle tickets, printing, carpet offcuts, lucky heather, televisions, knife sets, soul redemption, rating assessment appeals, and – more than all of the others put together – advertising.

Philosophically I tend to agree with George Orwell's comment that advertising is like the rattling of a stick in a swill bucket, and so I initially restricted my own activities to a dissembling-of-information kind of thing. Basically, that meant a new takeaway menu distributed regularly to every house in town by teenagers (with dire warnings ringing in their ears about what I'd do to them if piles of menus turned up in hedges, bins or postboxes). Still, I listened with an indulgent scepticism to the advertising salespeople who came to enliven my quiet afternoons with talk of how a modest ad on, say, the back door of the school minibus, or the town map, would finally swing the public round and quadruple turnover.

The long, quiet stretches of next to no customers were, however, becoming worrying, as were the calls from the Royal Mail complaining about postboxes filled with my menus. Of course, I reflected, not every business needs to advertise. The local Chinese takeaway or fish and chip shops never bothered. We didn't get leaflets through the door saying, 'Pancake Rolls; Buy one, get one free!' or the fish shop announcing, 'Now serving cod, haddock and huss! Also, chips! Special today: 10% off pickled onions, now only 9p!'

The difference, I supposed, was that these types of food have innate brand awareness. You always know exactly what you're going to get with a local Chinese or fish and chip shop: they're always there, always the same, and you either want them or you don't. But we had confused the customer by being much harder to pigeonhole. What, after all, is a diner? Is it a greasy spoon, or a restaurant, or like a Wimpy? Perhaps it was time to try this advertising game?

The way I began to see it was that a small blast of advertising would act like the suction part of a siphon. Once a certain number had been enticed up the hill to enjoy our meals, the others would follow in a constant stream. All I needed to do was choose the right media. Almost as if he had read my thoughts, an account manager from Wealdwide TV walked into my premises with the offer of producing my very own TV advert.

Wow, a TV advert!

It wouldn't be on television, of course – at least not television   89
as most of us know it. No, it would be shown on a TV set in the Uckfield Leisure Centre reception area, in their customer canteen and maybe the changing rooms. They would set up large screens and rotate a streamed selection of TV-style adverts for local companies, along with news of upcoming events at the leisure centre. It's a testament to the powers of the salesman that he managed to make all this sound bold and exciting.

Astute businesspeople might have realised from the start that the concept was flawed. I, however, made the mistake of working it all out on paper, analysing each market the ad could potentially reach, then the age range of people using the leisure centre, and what other cafés were within walking distance. The sales rep had been so very persuasive. He parried my argument that it all sounded a bit, well, mundane, by pointing out that it is in just such depressing environments that potential customers are in the frame of mind to be seduced by the kind of glamour the Diner offered.

'Of course it's mundane,' he chuckled, 'it's the municipal exercise facility, for heaven's sake!' But new thinking in advertising, he explained, was to lob adverts, grenade-like, into places where they were least expected. So you wouldn't advertise your new range of trendy jeans on MTV – oh dear, no! Who's going to notice them? No, you advertise them in the quiet afternoons during *Watercolour Challenge*, amid the funeral savings plans and walk-in baths. Thus achieving the 'Eh? What? Factor'. Before long I was frantically rushing around trying to find my cheque-book lest the salesman find someone else to take the space, while stopping occasionally to check camera angles through an imaginary lens made from my fingers.

Over the following weeks I discussed the content of the ad with my TV-writing brother and developed some ideas for the script. I decided to go with the effect of a handheld video camera, faux-amateurish style as if I'd filmed it myself; not dissimilar, in fact, to the one that he'd used in the opening credits of his own TV series. This was a big mistake, as the line between 'faux-amateurish' (in an ironic sort of way) and 'total crap' is extremely fine, and we crossed it easily.

The narrated script was meant to convey the cosy feeling of the Diner, while cunningly addressing the objections that people might have about coming into the restaurant (up a hill, yobs, burgers, coming in) and placing a firm emphasis on the healthy options. For example, cue voice of sultry woman:

There's always lots to enjoy at the Maximum Diner: plump burgers, the best hash browns in the Weald, frighteningly crisp salads and mouthwatering drinks.

Christopher, the proprietor, even keeps a cupboard of vegetarian food in case any vegetarians arrive... and there's a takeaway service if you can't stay for any reason...

There would be various acting 'parts' (happy family, attractive staff member, lovable yob), which I doled out to colleagues and friends, and we held a little rehearsal to iron out any technical glitches on our part. Then we waited for the TV crew.

It didn't arrive. Instead, a tall leathery-faced bloke turned up, sporting lopsided sunglasses and a very small camera. I asked him when the make-up lady was coming and he laughed himself into a coughing fit. Then he looked at the script and at the cast, all of us slightly less keen and expectant than at rehearsal, and started muttering defensively about 'not being bloody Tarantino'. He next tried to shoot the whole thing in one take, assuring me it would all be put right in the editing. We fell out as I insisted on at least two takes.

The resulting video was sent to me a few weeks later and was beyond embarrassing. It not only looked naff, but they'd set it to barrel organ music, with a voiceover by some kind of pantomime dame ('because we couldn't find a sultry enough lady'). Thankfully the staff at the leisure centre got bored of the screens after the first hour or two and turned them to face the wall for the remainder of the two-year contract.

Wealdwide TV left me with a chastened regard for advertising salesmen (and Tarantino) and hardly a bean for promotion. So we took brand promotion into our own hands and launched a T-shirt slogan competition. The prize for whoever came up with our winning slogan would be a free burger every day for a year. That's not as generous as it sounds, because it was unlikely that anyone was going to come in more than once or twice a week, and the cost price anyway was negligible.

The competition was enthusiastically embraced by everyone at the Diner and to kick things off we printed up new staff T-shirts with ideas of our own: 'Maximum Diner–Somewhere To Eat' and (I was quite proud of this) 'Maximum Diner–Say Hello to Mr Tasty'. Unfortunately some girls looking at my pale, over-worked face, thought it immensely funny to mistake the T-shirt for 'Say Hello to Mr Pasty', and to greet me hilariously with a 'Hello Mr Pasty' every time they came in or passed me in the High Street.

Nevertheless, we persevered and the entries rolled in, some of them quite interesting. God knows, I'd love to have used 'The Burgers Taste Even Nicer Than My Boyfriend's Dick', or even 'Maximum Diner–We Shit on Toppers'. My favourite of the lot was by an angry young goth, one of the town's arty kids, who came up with 'Maximum Diner–The Only Place Worth Going to in Yuckfield'. But the eventual winner was 'Open Your Mouth and Shovel It In', submitted by someone who conveniently lived in Eastbourne and was visiting for the day. Over the following year he made a weekly trip with his fiancée and various mates, spending generously on beers and additional items, and we became firm friends.

The Joy of Cooking

THE BEAUTY OF THE DINER CONCEPT is that people can just come along when they like. There are no bookings, no set lunch and dinner times, no 'I'm sorry, it's three-thirty so the kitchen is closed now.' At the Maximum Diner you could order virtually anything off the menu at any time from 9.01am to 11.59pm. So on top of the stress of not making quite enough money to keep up with the bills, there were worries about the unpredictability of demand. The post-pub hours still tended to be hyper-stressed, finding me cooking like a madman and throwing food onto the hatch. Then in the mornings and afternoons I might be sitting at the till, polishing the buttons or endlessly re-counting the same small change, when all of a sudden the First Uckfield Beavers turned up en masse for milkshakes, or the office two doors down decided to cram in for a team-building lunch.

Sometimes I was able to be positive about the long, quiet stretches. They were an excellent opportunity to catch up on all

93

the exciting details of Darren's wedding plans, and think up even more efficient ways of coping with a sudden busy afternoon. At more depressed, glass-half-empty sort of times, though, I pined to be curled up with a brand new girlfriend in front of the telly, or out with old friends enjoying a snack before a movie. I was starting to feel that the quiet evenings were just too boring and the busy late nights just too stressful.

Another reason why the quiet patches were hard to get through was that I missed the cooking. I'd never felt particularly drawn to the mechanics of cooking before, but there were parts of it, the mundane repetitive tasks, that I found surprisingly calming, spiritual almost. Gradually I got hooked.

I should have remembered this effect from my first catering job, cruising round the Caribbean on the MS *Celebration*. For the first two days of my kitchen training I was put in charge of peeling carrots, to be cut into little crudité batons by the Haitian chap next to me. Happy days! They gave me a fantastic peeler, great carrots and the days whizzed past in an exhilarating blur of thin orange slivers. Truth to tell, I was a bit disappointed when they moved me up to trimming celery on Day Three, but before long that celery was working its own green, crunchy magic on me. Then it was on to radishes, where, I'm afraid, the glamour faded. There was something faintly disheartening about cutting radishes into shapes so the passengers could point at them and say, 'Oh, my, don't those radishes look just like little flowers.'

94   But now, over ten years later, I found I was getting the old buzz back from cooking a Big Max. When the order went on the rack I'd grab the burger – a thick disc of raw, red meat – from the fridge and slam it on the new charcoal griddle. After a couple of minutes the edges would start to creep in a little and I'd see it browning underneath. With a swift movement of the spatula I'd flick it over and a burst of flames two feet high would flash from the charcoal as the fat hit it, bursting into blue smoke that gave

the burgers their unique barbecue flavour. I'd add two rashers of bacon to the griddle, where they'd instantly start to sizzle and brown. Grabbing a bun I'd throw it under the eye-level grill and then flick the burger ninety degrees to create a grid pattern – four beautiful brown lines from the bars of the griddle – on the burger, now seared and juicy, and almost ready.

With experience borne out of hundreds of toasted buns I'd grab the bun from under the grill at the exact second it was about to go from perfectly toasted to slightly burnt, and spoon a large dollop of creamy mayonnaise on the bottom half, give it a quick schmeer round and then chuck on a little pile of thinly sliced red onion, a mini-mountain of shredded iceberg lettuce, a perfect slice of beef tomato and a sliver of gherkin (I know not everyone likes gherkin, but to the purist a burger without it is like a roast without gravy). Another deft flick of the spatula and the two rashers of smoky bacon would be on top of the burger, cuddling up together like sweaty lovers. Above them would go a thickly cut slice of cheddar; then under the grill until the cheese would start to bubble and melt over the bacon like a duvet, then onto the pile of salad on the base of the bun.

A quick slather of barbecue sauce under the top of the bun and the Big Max would be done. A cocktail stick stuck in to hold everything in place, and then onto a large white plate – heavy duty, like the burgers. Thick-cut, fresh, golden-brown chips on the side and a large dollop of home-made, extra-creamy coleslaw, *et voilà*, onto the hatch and it's off to the customer.

It was skilled, it was fun, but alas, you only got to do it when customers came in. Actually, my major caveat about the joy of cooking is that, like having sex or watching *Fame Academy*, it's a lot less fun on your own. There are few things more tragic, more Alan Bennetty, than a single bloke cooking, say, a small roast chicken for himself (with roast potatoes, maybe another vegetable, possibly bread sauce and gravy), then eating it, all on his own. Then quietly doing the washing up, and sighing as he does the dishes with a Queen Mother Centenary tea towel, then... well, you get the picture.

Perhaps that's why we eat so much fast food in this country, because so many of us now live single lives, able to kid ourselves that we're 'choosy' or 'fiercely independent' – until it comes to dinner time, when the pathos of cooking alone rushes in and threatens to drown us, like cold gravy flopping onto a rather hard potato. It's easier to keep up the pretence with a takeout.

I used to have a secret desire to live in a commune, or go back to the seventh century (which is about as likely), to a place where everyone mucks in, shares out the chores, then sleeps together in a long house. I mean longhouse. Two people cooking together can be quite cosy, three is fun, four is a party. Five is getting a bit Amish. Obviously there comes a point at which there are too many people cooking, and the broth starts to suffer, but those occasions are few and far between. I found myself musing that community cooking, like the giant paella-making festivals in Spain, could catch on in Britain, though perhaps not with a dish containing squid and not in the great outdoors.

It was just an idea, though. It didn't mean that I wanted to share my own kitchen in Uckfield with a leading Spanish *haute cuisine* chef.

Cristina had rung from Spain with a favour to ask. She'd started going out with a chef from a hotel in Barcelona and this new boyfriend, Antonio, wanted to come and extend his culinary artistry in the most exciting place in the world for cooking.

'What? Uckfield?' I asked, surprised.

'No, London, of course. But his English is so *mierda* I thought you might have him first. He could help you cook at the Diner, and you could teach him English. Please, Chris? It would only be for a few days and he doesn't even have to stay with you.'

Great, I thought. I get to spend my working hours with some Spanish guy, communicating in grunts, while he puts prissy hotel-style sprigs of parsley on all the food. It was always like this when Christina introduced her new boyfriends – I could never quite overcome that initial fit of pique. But a couple of weeks later Antonio arrived. He came to Sussex having spent the weekend at a specialist cookery bookshop in London. He had been all weekend in one small shop, leaving only to eat alone in expensive restaurants, gathering ideas (as chefs like to put it).

Antonio was a serious-looking man, well groomed, with short dark hair, in his mid-thirties. He seemed quite placid for a chef, with a permanently thoughtful expression as though he was turning menu ideas over in his mind, or trying to imagine tastes and combinations of flavours. The plan was for him to drive over from a friend's house in Lewes and spend a few hours a day for the next week helping out in the Diner, while learning everything I could teach him about culinary English. Guessing that The Three Garys had no real vocation as teaching assistants, I suggested he came along for the quiet patch of the day between breakfast and lunch. This was also the time when I tended to have the shift to myself.

The next morning we arrived at the Diner together – me in my 'Open Your Mouth and Shovel It In' T-shirt, Antonio in his starched whites, blue checked trousers and neckerchief. I told him the formal uniform wouldn't be strictly necessary, but he looked at me with the mournful expression and gave a little shrug. I wasn't sure if that meant he didn't understand but didn't like to admit it, or he did understand but preferred to do things his way, or neither. So I gave a little shrug back and we went inside. I wondered what the locals would say when they saw a proper chef cooking their chicken nuggets and chips.

97

Fond as I was of Cristina, I didn't really want her boyfriend in my diner. First, it was excruciatingly embarrassing to have to mime instructions in public, and secondly the cooking at the Diner might not be complicated but it had to be done very fast. Hotel chefs are all very well at churning out breakfast buffet food, or artfully arranged trays of sandwiches, but I didn't think he'd be much use when it came to the organised chaos of a short-order restaurant. Thirdly, I had tried teaching people English before and was rubbish at it, being surprised to discover that an ability to speak English is only one of the more basic skills required to get the language across. Still, at least Antonio could chop things. I could always leave him chopping stuff in the back while I did the fancy stuff out front.

Entering the Diner, Antonio walked straight into the kitchen and stood there, hands on hips, surveying the pieces of junk that I liked to call equipment. He seemed particularly interested in the griddle arrangement that the blacksmith had rigged up for me, looking at it from all angles, bending down to examine it from underneath, then gingerly lifting up one side and nosing around underneath. He rattled it experimentally while I stood on the other side of the counter watching him, quietly dying of shame. If you think that's bad, I thought, wait till you see the fridges. On the plus side, there was always the possibility that he'd throw a Gordon Ramsay-style tantrum and clear off.

Instead of which, Antonio stopped examining the griddle and turned to me with a big smile. 'Is very good. Very clever. *Bueno.*' I'm not sure if they have sarcasm in Spain, so I gave him the benefit of the doubt.

'Yeah, does the job,' I said. 'It's my own design.'

Antonio looked at me expectantly. 'Wha' can I do?' he asked, very slowly.

So I set him to work peeling and preparing the potatoes for hash, then shredding lettuce, slicing tomatoes, chopping onions, mixing coleslaw and making little salads. With each item of food I went over the English for the word several times, until he got it right. Monday mornings are never very busy and normally I would enjoy doing the chopping myself, so as consolation I settled down with the newspaper, after teaching Antonio about that great British delicacy, the bacon sandwich.

Whenever he finished chopping any item, which he did rather quickly, he popped his head over the counter and said, 'Another bacon sandweedge Chris, con soss tomard?'

'Ah no, Antonio,' I would correct him, 'The phrase is "tomato ketchup". TOMATO KETCHUP.'

'Tomarrr Kechoop.'

'Toma-TO Ketchup.'

'Tomarrrr-tow kechoop.'

'Exactly, Antonio. And yes, I'd love one, thank you.' I returned to the paper, to the chant of 'Tomarr-TOW kechoop, tomarr-TOW kechoop, tomarr...' from the kitchen.

As opening time approached, Antonio retied his neckerchief, put on a clean apron and checked himself in the mirror. When customers started wondering in, some did a quick double-take on seeing Antonio smiling at them with a fixed grin, as though he were being presented to the Queen after cooking her lunch. I felt immediately defensive, saying, 'He's from Spain', to everyone, as if that could explain anything. But comments were all complimentary anyway, along the lines of 'Going a bit upmarket aren't we, Chris?'

Over the next couple of days I grew quite fond of Antonio. He turned out to be fantastic in the kitchen, and during conversations I discovered that he earned about five times more than me, as executive chef of a five-star hotel. To fill in the quieter hours,

99

Antonio hired a car and toured East Sussex to try out the catering options. He took an interest in everything to do with food, from service station sandwiches to sweet shops to teashops, and often returned puzzled or outraged at the things that pass for food in some of these places. Though I felt I should defend our native cuisine, there was no explaining or excusing garage-bought sandwiches, which Antonio described as being like a slimy dead thing in semi-frozen bread.

The English lessons went pretty well too, as I was surprised to discover just what a limited language we get away with in a kitchen. Bigger; smaller; hotter; more cooked; on top; ooh, no cut that bit off, they're bound to notice: that just about covers it. In fact, after scarcely more than a week, Antonio came over and said he thought he could move on.

'But I haven't taught you how to do the fillet o' fish burgers yet!' I protested. Nevertheless, he said time was limited, and asked if I knew Anton Edelmann at the Savoy Hotel.

'Do I know Anton Edelmann? Do I know Anton Edelmann? *Maître chef des cuisines* for twenty years at the Savoy, teacher and mentor to many of the best chefs in the world, publisher of a dozen books on the theory and practice of cooking? Of course I don't bloody know Anton Edelmann.'

Antonio pushed a piece of paper into my hand with the Savoy's phone number on it and asked if I would call it, and tell Mr Edelmann that Philippe at the Hotel Arts, Barcelona, would vouch for him. So I rang the Savoy but could only get as far as his third most senior PA, who said: 'Maximum Diner? Where was that again? I'm not sure that I've heard of...'

'Ah, well, we're a little out in the sticks, ha ha.'

'Hmm, I know most country restaurants...'

'Look, just tell Anton that Antonio is here, will you? Antonio from the Hotel Arts, Barcelona.' And I rang off. 'Bloody metropolitans.'

Within ten minutes the phone rang. It was Mr Edelmann's first most senior PA with a message for Señor Antonio. Mr Edelmann would be delighted to have him join him at the Savoy, and would that very evening be too soon?

The whole 17.5%

THE PROFIT GRAPH OF A NEW BUSINESS is supposed to plunge straight down, breaking through into the loss portion before bottoming out seductively, then climbing slowly but surely into profit and ever upwards. The idea is that, in order to develop a good strong business, firm foundations need to be laid, and that means you not only won't but shouldn't make any money to start off with. Anyone can rip a few people off to make a quick buck, with rotten service and cheap, nasty food, but unless your diner is on wheels you'll soon run out of suckers.

Over the first year of trade the Maximum Diner profitability graph had slumped very nicely indeed – almost a textbook example – but over the following eighteen months it was proving a little tardy in coming back up. When this happens what you try and do is spend your way out, indeed what other option is there? Given a lack of customers the natural inclination is to go out and get them, but all the obvious methods of doing that are impossible when you not only don't have any money, but have a pile of bills bursting out of files and drawers, demanding your attention. As I'd already learnt, any type of advertising, even just getting a blackboard to go outside on the pavement, costs surprising amounts of money, which has to be weighed against paying the wages, or getting a delivery of potatoes. Catch-22. You can't afford to get customers in because you don't have enough customers. Faced with this problem, many small businesses dip into their VAT savings.

VAT is meant to be a tax on what people spend, but from a trader's point of view it seems like a tax on your business. For each portion of chips sold at, say, £1.15, the Chancellor was getting 15p and I was getting, well, nothing at all – once the cost of wages, insurance, rent, rates, bank charges, potatoes and oil had been totted up. Not only was this making life very hard, but it was holding the Maximum Diner back from becoming the brand it could be. In the meantime I had several thousands of pounds of VAT money sitting around doing nothing but waiting to be paid to the government.

Since it was legally mine until the day each quarter when it was due to be paid over, I dipped into it. Soon the 'dipping' became outright spending, much of it on menu leafleting. I was gambling that sales would increase enough to repay it before the money became due, a bit like Arthur Fowler and the *EastEnders* Christmas Club money. There's bound to come a time in every 103 small business, I reasoned, when they must make the choice of remaining small and insignificant, or reaching up and plucking the fruit of opportunity from the tree. And if they have to use someone else's ladder to reach up to that tree, then so be it. So, I nicked the ladder and the tree turned out to be a telegraph pole.

Before long, the VAT bailiff made a visit. He was called Mr Sweet which, in other circumstances, I might have found interestingly ironic. Mr Sweet was a mountain of a man with an Amish-style chinstrap beard and a glass eye. Had he and Hagrid from Burger Off got together, they would have made a terrific tag wrestling team (as Sweet and Unsavoury, maybe). Anyway, he did a thorough stocktake of the business's movable possessions and charged me an additional £120 for the privilege.

Although this was an absolute calamity, I was determined not to get oh-so-predictably tetchy. Poor Mr Sweet must get very tired of listening to rotten business failures making carping, sarcastic comments when he's only doing his job, and I thought, no, I'll maintain my dignity. The government has to raise money to spend on hospitals and schools and therefore needs an enforcement procedure, so we'll conduct this sad but necessary duty in a spirit of respectfulness and harmony. Becky offered to spit in his tea but I refused to let her. 'No. Becky,' I said, 'No. No. No... Oh. alright then. If you must.'

Mr Sweet informed me that I had ten days to pay what I owed plus his fee, after which he'd be back to collect my stuff. And that would have been that. I would have gone under. The Maximum Diner would have been sold from under me.

I could perhaps have gone back to my brother at this stage, and asked to borrow a bit more, but how could I assure him that this wouldn't happen again in three or, maybe six, months' time? We had customers, we had skilled staff and good food, and yet we couldn't seem to get the margins right. All I'd be able to show for the extra money would be a regular family appearance as the Useless Sibling That Everyone Has to Help Out All The Time. Somehow that didn't sound gratifying enough.

Then Ken who ran the café-kiosk at Brighton Marina made a chance observation that altered my life. He told me I'd been overpaying my VAT.

Just after opening the Diner I'd moved to live near Brighton Marina, renting what the estate agent called a Yachtsman's Cottage – a misleading name that conjures images of a smallish house with more excuse than most to call itself 'Seaview'. In fact it was a glorified beach hut, with scary vacuum-assisted plumbing. But it was the best I could afford and I loved it. The cottage had a freshness about it – the gulls, the seaspray, boats dipping beside the jetty – that acted as an antidote to all my troubles at the Diner.

Except that one of my new troubles was that I was going to have to give up the cottage to help pay off my debts.

I wouldn't have minded so much had it been winter, when to avoid hypothermia you had to batten down the hatches against icy horizontal rain, a wind-chill of minus 20 and vast waves bashing the jetty against the metal pillars that anchored it to the sea bed. In winter I would have happily swapped it for a bedsit in Uckfield, but this was May, and an early summer sun was glinting off the water and brightening the fibreglass decks. Had I felt up to it, I might have shouted a cheery 'Ahoy' to the sailors queuing up to use the marina washing machines. Instead, I dragged myself off to a small kiosk at the end of the marina to borrow a cup of coffee and a fag from Ken.

Ken was reputed to have downshifted, as we now say, from a career in the City to making bacon sandwiches on the marina seawall, and he was one of those few people with whom I could have a proper chat about small-time catering. No topic was too dull for us to pick over, setting the world to rights re plastic fork designs; napkins (two-ply, or single, which to choose?); relish, chutney and pickle (is there any technical distinction, and why do people keep them in the fridge anyway these days?). There was a certain element of professional rivalry and one-upmanship in our chats and, frankly, I sometimes found his attitude a bit patronising for a man in a kiosk. But I let it go.

105

That day, Ken listened sympathetically to my account of the VAT catastrophe before asking, 'So how much of your sales were you actually paying that VAT on?'

'Durrr, all of it, obviously,' I replied.

'But you shouldn't have been, you great pillock,' he announced. 'Food sold for consumption off the premises, if served cold, is designated zero-rated. You charge VAT *only* on the hot food. Don't you know anything? I thought you had a bit of experience in this trade.'

'Yeah, well! At least I have a proper café and not some windy shed covered in seagull shit,' I began to respond; but it came out instead as, 'Yeah well! At least... Bloody hell, that's BRIL-LIANT!!' Then, after a hurried exchange about the exact VAT notices to look for, and a high-five over the mustard bottles, I sprinted home to get my calculator.

When I had opened the Diner my accountant, Mr Burridge, had patiently explained that VAT was payable on everything I sold unless it required no processing whatsoever and was takeaway. So, for example, an apple wouldn't attract VAT if it were simply sold as a whole apple, to take away. But if that apple was eaten in, or sliced up and made into an apple pie, or indeed a strudel, crumble or apple sauce, or if it was turned over, baked, pulped, fermented, frittered, put on a stick and dipped in toffee or stuffed into the mouth of a baby pig and roast on a spit, then I would have to add 17.5 percent onto the price. Eat in or take-away, cold or hot, I would have to pay that extra money back to Her Majesty's Customs and Excise every quarter.

At least that's what Mr Burridge told me, as indeed did the VAT inspector who was sent round to check my books just after I had begun trading. But it seemed they had both got it crucially

106

wrong. It didn't matter if the food was processed, so long as it wasn't hot when the customer got it. Back at my cottage-hut (huttage?), I frantically bashed at the buttons on the calculator. For every milkshake, salad, coleslaw, dip, mineral water, sandwich, pudding and many others that I had sold takeaway or delivery since opening, I was entitled to get back nearly a fifth of the selling price. The VAT man owed me... thousands and thousands of pounds.

This changed everything. For the whole two years of financial hardship and despair, when I had believed we were losing money, we had in truth been a profitable company. Not very profitable, maybe, but profitability (like virginity) is something you either have or you don't.

I had two immediate questions: would they give the money back, and would my brother loan me some of the money owing while I waited? I got a quick yes to the latter, but the former was squarely in the lap of the apparatchiks at Customs and Excise.

My accountant, Mr Burridge, would have been the man to sort all this out. Although he would come across as a bit like Private Godfrey in *Dad's Army* – kindly and slightly perplexed by modern life – he had a keen mind, drove a brand new, top of the range Porsche and had a much younger wife, who looked like Meg Ryan. Unfortunately, he was unavailable, having chosen to wind down his business, citing the stress of accounting. Stress? Accountancy? The Three Garys and I could tell him a thing or two about stress. Still, it was hard to get cross with a man who was off work with stress, so my ire was directed at Her Majesty's representative, a Miss Feltham.

Had you known nothing of Mr Burridge's Meg Ryan inclinations, and had watched him and Miss Feltham in a special 'accountants only' edition of *Blind Date* you might have paired the two of them off. She was a slightly more feminine version of Mrs Doubtfire, with something of the Widdecombe about her.

Fortunately for Meg, they were doomed never to meet, and I had to face Miss Feltham alone.

I had arranged to see her on a Monday morning so that we could concentrate without interruption from any customers, and she arrived on the doorstep at 9am sharp at the beginning of a warm June day. 'VAT is payable on all takeaway food,' she said from the doorstep, grimly clutching a briefcase and making no effort to come inside.

'No,' I said gently, not wanting to show up her ignorance. 'I'm afraid VAT isn't payable on cold takeaway food.'

'Yes it is,' she said, still on the doorstep. It would have been a mysterious exchange for any passer-by to overhear.

I pulled out the Customs and Excise Notice 709/2, concerning value added tax and food, which Mr Burridge had found behind a cupboard somewhere and sent to me. I had highlighted certain sections of this, and held them out for Miss Feltham to read. She scanned the page silently.

'I'd better come in,' she concluded.

When accountants want a laugh, they possibly reach for Customs and Excise Notice 709/2, a dull green A5 pamphlet. It details the latest pronouncement on which foods have no VAT payable on it (in other words is zero-rated) and which have. Essentially, cold food and drinks for consumption off the premises is zero-rated, but there are certain exceptions. Fizzy drinks are VATable, milky drinks are zero-rated. Why? I don't know. No one does. However, I like to imagine the Chancellor of the Exchequer way back when, announcing the plans to the PM and his colleagues around the Cabinet table: 'Fair's fair. I'll let the milkshakes go, but I'll be buggered if I let them have the lemonade tax-free.'

Chocolate cake isn't VATable, chocolate biscuits are, but it depends on whether the chocolate covering completely surrounds the cake. Confused? McVities were, and they fought a long legal battle with Customs and Excise over the issue of Jaffa Cakes. Customs and Excise insisted they were a biscuit cynically misnamed to avoid paying tax. The VAT tribunal went over issues of packaging, where in a supermarket they were kept (ie cake aisle or biscuit aisle), and size. Size mattered; so much so that McVities made a birthday-cake-sized one and brought it along to the tribunal. Another crucial issue raised was texture: cakes go hard when they are stale, biscuits go soft. Jaffa Cakes go hard; ergo, they're a cake. In the end, McVities won: Jaffa Cakes are cakes, which may come as a surprise to Britain's dunking public, but The Law has spoken.

Where part of the product is cold and part is hot, the whole item is deemed to be VATable if it is packaged all together. So a baked potato filled with coleslaw is entirely VATable unless the coleslaw is sold separately, in which case an allowance must be made for how much each contributes toward the end selling price. But, just suppose the butter for the potato is in a little foil wrapper handed over separately, rather than in a knob, as it were, stuck in the potato. Can you claim back the contribution this makes to the selling price? No one knows; it's one of the many imponderables.

I could go on. Shall I go on? Sandwiches are a minefield. Egg mayonnaise and bacon sandwich zero-rated, bacon sandwich VATable, unless it's gone cold. Also critical is the purpose of the heating process, as became clear in the case of The Great American Bagel Factory.

The bagel people weren't charging VAT on their toasted takeaway bagels because they claimed they were cold when sold. Customs and Excise claimed, not unreasonably, that toasting the bagels made them hot, and hot food is VATable, and demanded tens of thousands of pounds in back taxes. Clearly The Great American Bagel Factory couldn't round up all their takeaway customers, tell them they'd made a mistake and ask them to pay the VAT, so they faced being bankrupted, if they lost.

After several years the case came to court, where TGABF's defence was that the bagels were indeed toasted, but only in order to change the texture, as they were cold by the time the customer ate them. The wise judge – after perhaps enquiring, 'And what, might I ask, is a Bay Gel?' and on being informed by the usher, perhaps exclaiming, 'Well I never, what will they think of next!' – ordered an adjournment while an order of bagels was sent out for. Result? The judge found for the bagel people, and bagel purveyors rejoiced throughout the land.

Seeing the attitude of Miss Feltham it was clear how such a case could drag on. She seemed to have a Sheriff of Nottingham complex about collecting as much tax as possible, combined with a very sketchy and muddle-headed knowledge of the VAT rules themselves. But perhaps Customs and Excise find their own leaflets so boring they can't even be bothered to read them, and simply make up the rules as they go along. Perhaps they're not the right people for the job: it's odd, if you think about it, to have your tax assessed by the same people who check your car boot for brandy or 'dirty' bombs at the ferry terminal.

Certainly, faced with the evidence of her own pamphlet, I had Miss Feltham on the ropes. She went to the phone, had a long chat with her supervisor, came back to the table, squeezed herself into the booth, opened her briefcase, took out a calculator, a nice fresh pad, a selection of pens in different colours, a rubber and a ruler, laid them all out carefully and said, 'Alright, then.'

It was time for the serious negotiating to start, and we kept at it right through the day, just the two of us, sitting at a table with piles of paper filled with calculations and yards and yards of old till roll. Till rolls only gave so much sales information, so a lot had to be bargained over. First, what percentage of sales were takeaway over each period, including the periods when we were not doing deliveries, and when we were. Then the percentages within each menu item. Then, precisely how much of each item we had sold. Negotiations went on, and on, and on, through the stifling heat of a warm summer's day. Then, just as I thought progress had finally been made, we had to reassess all of the information in the light of which season it occurred. As Miss Feltham helpfully pointed out while sipping her iced water, 'One does sell fewer cold things in the winter.'

At intervals, I tried to introduce the idea of compromise. 'I won't claim for the barbecue sauce that goes with the potato wedges,' I found myself saying, 'if you'll forget the chocolate puddings that we serve with ice cream.' But these conciliatory gestures were taken as cause for further probing: 'Ice cream? Packaged with the cake or on the side? Because, if it's in the same box, I'll have to reassess all the calculations we made about cake in the light of this information you're now supplying me with.'

Okay, I decided, if she was going to be petty, then I'd show her petty, and demanded that an allowance of 5p be made for the little sachets of salt that went with each portion of chips. Strictly speaking, you can't do that – oh, it's been tried – but she didn't know that condiments had their own separate regulations, and seemed quite alarmed for a while, before I relented and went back to stabbing the side of my hand with a biro.

Mind games? It was Spassky and Fischer all over again. It was the chess scene in *The Thomas Crown Affair*, only without the sexual chemistry. As the hours ticked on I began to feel convinced that I'd be locked in combat over the till rolls with Miss Feltham for the rest of my reproductive years. I grew desperate to leave her to it and go and find some FUN. But I remembered the first rule of business: never, ever, turn your back on a VAT inspector. And eventually it was over, as Miss Feltham woke me from my reverie with the snap of her briefcase closing. 'We'll be in touch', she said frostily, and disappeared into the evening sunshine.

Like the psycho in a horror film who just won't die, Miss Feltham returned for one last battle. She telephoned to say that my multi-thousand-pound rebate was off, since 'outside catering is classed as eating in and therefore VAT is payable on every-thing'. I felt like weeping, as I tried to reason with her that a lone takeaway sandwich is not outside catering. Surely she could see, that lots of sandwiches on a platter, with the pointy bits all stick-ing upwards and an artistic sprinkling of watercress and cherry tomatoes over them, delivered to an office leaving party, is out-side catering? But just because the catering is taken outside, it isn't necessarily outside catering. So that's the stress that my accountant had been talking about.

Finally, though, Mr Burridge came through for me. He had returned to work for a last swan song and took it upon himself to ring Miss Feltham's boss and demand he call the dogs off. I got my refund, paid back the interim loan from my brother and settled down to enjoy life on the right side of the graph.

Love and money

OVER THE PREVIOUS MONTHS OF FINANCIAL CRISIS I had always been honest and upfront with the staff about the precarious nature of the business, the 'difficult trading circumstances' and our cash-flow problems. We were in it together was the message I hoped to get across.

Or at least some of us were, for Darren had handed in his notice. It was, he explained, nothing personal, just a simple case of correcting a false move in his career. He was an ambitious lad and had clearly calculated that the Maximum Diner wasn't going to make him rich any time soon. Instead he put his faith in Amway, the American brand of pyramid-selling cleaning products. He had begun selling it before he left us. Indeed, he nagged me so hard for a contract that I gave in and within a month had a greater variety of cleaning fluids than alcoholic drinks (though some could probably double for both). We also lost the use of most of our storeroom space as he took to dismantling parts of the oven and extractor fan and dunking them in dustbins full of expensive suds, where he'd leave them for days, 'deep cleaning' he would call it, though it looked like 'festering' to the rest of us.

The key to immense wealth with Amway is not to sell the stuff yourself, but to recruit other people to sell it for you. You are then entitled to a percentage of what your recruits sell, and of what the people they recruit sell, and so on. In theory you can get very rich. In practice, Darren ended up pissing everybody off, as he endlessly tried to bully people into joining the club. There was absolutely no subject that he couldn't turn to improved cleaning methods – if your entire family had just been wiped out by a falling meteorite, he'd have a detergent to recommend for the tombstones, and a few suggestions of how to bring in new clients while visiting the cemetery. There was a huge collective sigh of relief when he left.

Not so with Becky. We were all a bit depressed when she threw in her job – especially me, as I felt partly to blame.

The problems began when Lee, Becky's unlovely boyfriend, started coming in on her shifts to check she wasn't talking to other men. Not an ideal situation, as he would sit at the counter staring sourly at any male customer over the age of twelve and, worse than that, would help himself to large quantities of lager on the house. Realising that Becky was being led astray by an older boyfriend, I took her quietly to one side and told her that I'd turn a blind eye about the bottles he'd had so far but that he really had to start paying for anything he drank.

You should never overestimate the loyalty of your staff. Becky immediately told Lee that I'd accused them both of stealing and he stormed into the kitchen to confront me. He grabbed a Pyrex jug and brandished it menacingly, threatening to 'cut' me. I tried to placate him with claims that I'd been misquoted: 'Stealing? no mate, I meant er... borrowing. You've been borrowing lager, that's what I meant!', while from the corner of my eye I surveyed my range of weapons. These included cucumbers, a whisk and several frozen burgers. Sure, the knives were not too far off, but since Lee hadn't actually opted for anything metal or sharp yet it seemed silly to escalate matters. Becky dragged him away, though, screaming, a bit hurtfully, that I 'wasn't worth it'.

I employed a new waitress called Sophie. She was blonde and beautiful with a deep voice like Clarissa Dickson Wright and an unguarded friendliness that on any other person would sound like dementia. Customers found Sophie charming, but unnerving. Coming into the shop they would be assailed by a vision of loveliness who would launch earnestly into something like: 'That's a lovely shirt I love that shirt it goes very nicely with your trousers do you want to swap, what do you want to eat by the way do you want coffee yeah, nice coffee? Umm like your shoes too.' Then she'd wander off and forget to get your coffee.

Maybe it was the Sophie Effect but we were at last beginning to see an upturn in trade. I marked takings on a large graph in the back room. It was quite a work of art, with the day divided into sections: pre-lunch, lunch, late lunch, etc, and takings further subdivided into eat-in and takeaway. Heavy highlighting was used for any record-breaking sessions, and soon the chart started lighting up with bright patches, even if they were only for, say, 'busiest pre-lunch session on a Wednesday.'

The areas where we were doing best were Sunday breakfast (for reasons outlined earlier) and midweek late afternoons, as parents brought their children in for tea after school. However, older schoolchildren were also beginning to come in at lunchtimes, and pre-lunch was also picking up as people working in offices nearby pulled their lunchtimes forward in an attempt to avoid all the schoolkids. All this was encouraging, though the change in profits didn't seem hugely significant. There was also more of a workload, and with Darren gone and Sophie covering only part of Becky's job, I was back to working a sixteen-hour day.

An inconvenient time, then, to fall in love.

I met Naomi at a party. Not being able to go to parties until well after midnight meant that I would pitch up full of enthusiasm just as they were ending, along with the minicab drivers. For once, though, arriving late was a good move, as it meant that I was clutching the party's only palatable bottle of wine when I bumped into Naomi sitting on the stairs. Naomi had had a lousy evening and was happy to have a top-up. She was also drunk enough not to mind my smelling of burgers. After the simplest and briefest of chats, where she smiled her bright, toothy smile at me, clinked glasses, and laughed at a lame joke or two, she suggested I walk her home.

Naomi had a classic girl-next-door appeal to her – healthy, pretty and outdoorsy, her face framed with an attractive mop of brown curls. You could picture her in a headscarf, going out to milk cows, or singing 'Bringing in the Sheaves' at church on *Little House on the Prairie*. As if this wasn't terrific enough, she was an incredibly cool dancer with one of the best collections of Northern Soul music you'll ever come across south of Wigan. Not that she had much chance to indulge these tastes, being stuck on her own with two young children on an estate in Uckfield, trying hard to keep some spark alive while being plagued by an embittered ex-husband.

Uckfield, as well as being the 'settling-down' capital of East Sussex, is also the breaking-up capital. There are an awful lot of single, divorced mothers (and fathers). I had half hoped that the young mums might be a thriving and sociable market sector for the Diner, but since they have to rub along with about 57p a week disposable income, we did rather better with 'Dads with visiting rights' on Saturday mornings.

Over the following weeks Naomi and I grew increasingly fond of each other, within the confines of me working all the time and her juggling childcare with trying to get onto a teacher training access course. As soon as Catherine came to work I would shoot round to Naomi's house for an hour or two, and we would go out for a romantic afternoon tea, spoilt just a little by her six- and ten-year-olds' insistence on flanking their mum like junior bodyguards. Then, just as everyone had begun to relax and spread around the table a bit, there'd come a desperate call from Catherine to tell me she couldn't cope on her own and I'd have to usher the kids back into the van and rush to work. Later, I would go round after closing time for a cup of midnight hot chocolate, all hyped up after my long shift, to find Naomi half-asleep after her's.

This was ridiculous; I decided to close the Diner on Mondays.

Looking back I can see that this was one of the critical points in my career as a catering entrepreneur – the point at which I decided I wanted a life just as much as (and perhaps just a teeny bit more than) becoming the next Rocco Forte. You simply don't shut up shop for the day in the crowded world of the fast food industry if you want to keep any credibility. But I was enjoying myself too much to care, and not just with Naomi but also as 'Mum's boyfriend', waiting for the kids at the school gates, snatching defeat from the brink of victory at Monopoly, or whisking them off to the cinema. Of course there was always the luxury of retreating back to the Diner if family life got too tense but it felt good to have a regular guest spot in that household.

117

Spending time with Naomi also had a surprising effect on my worklife, prompting me to rethink my entire marketing strategy. Until then I'd been a zealous speculate-to-accumulate sort of guy, with a firm belief in improving the brand experience as a means of upping trade. Years of single motherhood, by contrast, had given Naomi a keen eye for saving money and gradually she began to win me round to her no-nonsense bottom-line, cost-cutting approach.

An early example was our battle over the popcorn machine. Naomi refused to understand my decision to 'invest' £200 (most of the week's net earnings) in acquiring this unnecessary object.

'It adds value to the eating experience,' I explained. 'You give customers a little bowl of popcorn when they arrive, and they think you're being really kind. But actually, the popcorn is a little salty and so they get thirsty and spend more on drinks.'

'No they don't,' argued Naomi. 'They're not that dim. They just get filled up with popcorn and order less food.'

I suggested that Naomi was failing somewhat to see the bigger picture and she retorted that I was failing to grasp elementary maths. It ended with a small argument and the popcorn machine being thrown into the garden. The next morning there was a giant popcorn tree stretching way up into the clouds... Okay, there wasn't; it rusted away while the growing weeds hid it from view.

Naomi had a point, though. It struck me for the first time since I opened the Diner that I was selling a premium, exclusive product at a fast food price – piling it low and selling it cheap as it were – which doesn't really work as a business model.

McDonald's, of course, do the opposite and sometimes price their food so low that it's hard to imagine how they make any profit at all. For instance, 79p for a cheeseburger must be perilously close to cost price. But they make their margin within the same meal by charging almost as much again for a cardboard cup of ice and Coke – which is, after all, just fizzy water with a couple of teaspoons of sugar and chemicals. At the other end of the scale a restaurant like The Ivy, say, might charge ten times that for a starter while using more or less the same amount of food as in the cheeseburger, but their labour costs will be proportionately much higher too.

Somehow I had managed to combine these two approaches by paying higher than average wages while scraping the barest minimum profit (with the exception of my loss leaders – which more than adequately performed their task of making losses). It was hard to know how to dig myself out of the morass. While my policy of paying staff high wages in return for greater loyalty hadn't entirely paid off with Becky or Darren, I'd have a rebellion to deal with if I tried trying to lower them now. Similarly, our customers had got used to low prices and, more to the point, I couldn't afford to reprint all the menus with higher prices on them. Classy menus, you see, more added value. And I could just imagine how the Garys would react to little stickers hiking up the prices of their favourite post-pub snacks.

The answer had to be increased turnover, but how could I achieve this in a diner with only five tables? It was Naomi who finally came up with the answer: home deliveries.

Night Riders

HOME DELIVERIES HAD OCCURRED TO ME in the past but I had assumed that there were good reasons why burger bars didn't do them. Specifically, I thought that chips and burgers would be a soggy mess after they'd sat in someone's car for twenty minutes while they tried to find a house in the dark. Evidently not, though, as we soon picked up regular customers who ordered weekly, daily even. One man even ordered twice a day, and asked if we could deliver at breakfast.

120   I had also half-imagined that we might lose all our takeaway trade, but that didn't happen either. And my belief that competition amongst fast food rivals was going to be a 'zero-sum game' – that if one place was to increase its trade by 10 percent, then their rivals must lose 10 percent – turned out to be wrong, too. In fact, the market for fast food seemed to be getting ever larger as more places opened. True, the old Starburger had bitten the dust, and the whole Mr Sweet episode had been a close run

thing, but when we started deliveries we didn't detract from our takeaway trade much – nor, as I discovered from chatting to the manager of Topper's, from their pizza/fondue deliveries. Of course, common sense dictates that someone must be losing out – McCains and their Micro-Chips, perhaps, or whoever makes Toast Toppers these days – but we hear so much about the rise in figures for obesity, that maybe there was no loser. Perhaps we really are just eating more and more as new food options appear, the market expanding along with our belts.

I had planned to nip out and do deliveries myself, but as turnover shot up 80 percent it was clear that we would need to employ drivers. Adam was the first to answer the hastily written appeal stuck up in the window. He was a Surfer Dude, which isn't an easy act to pull off in the middle of Sussex, fifteen miles from the sea. Undeterred, he'd got the full kit: Oakley's shades, No Fear T-shirt, loud shorts (weather permitting), Ocean Sports stickers on his Vauxhall Nova, and the requisite far-off look in the eye that spoke of an eternal search for the next big wave. We never saw much evidence of actual surfing – no tan, no salt- and sun-bleached hair – but surely no one would drive around delivering burgers with a surfboard rack strapped to the roof of their car just for effect. Would they?

Adam made it clear from the outset that the job was strictly temporary as he was saving up for a one-way flight to Malibu. He'd just left school and the world was his lobster, so to speak. But months passed and Adam never quite notched up enough money to book that ticket, though he happily poured scorn on his old schoolfriends pursuing careers as under-managers at Tesco's. Malibu's loss, though, was the Maximum Diner's gain. Adam was so likable and helpful that to point out that another season had gone by and he was still living with his mum and delivering burgers would have been churlish. Though I told tales about hitchhiking round America, and tried to articulate the joy of leaving home and travelling the world, Adam always listened carefully and then did the exact opposite. Perhaps the real reason he didn't leave Uckfield was something to do with the pretty girls waiting for him at the end of each shift, and though I explained that Malibu had girls too – indeed, California was noted for it – I think he felt he hadn't exhausted East Sussex's supply yet.

Delivery drivers are seen by some as the postal workers of the fast food industry, with all the attendant psychological problems that implies. They see themselves, on the other hand, as latterday Pony Express riders, and managers would do well to keep them in that positive frame of mind. I tried to foster a belief in Adam (it didn't take much fostering) that he was some kind of rebel loner, like a maverick undercover cop who plays by his own rules, or an American Indian scout, or the platoon sniper: part of the team, but always one step ahead of it. Sort of nomadic, too, with skin like tanned leather and eyes like chips of blue steel, seeking out those tricky house numbers.

Drivers usually have day jobs, and arrive to do deliveries in the evening already tired and fed up, so the game is on to try and make them feel special. And, since you can't see what they're up to most of the time, it's always a good idea to keep them happy, so if Adam saw himself more as Top Gun than Postman Pat that was fine by me.

It's also a good idea to make sure that delivery drivers are well fed before they start their shift. As a room service waiter I had discovered how many Duchesse potatoes or wafer-thin mints one can stuff in one's mouth between the lift doors closing by the kitchen on the ground floor and opening again by the VIP suite on the sixth. Ever since, I prefer to collect takeaway food myself, avoiding any possibility that the driver will stop down a dark alleyway and pick bits of pepperoni off my pizza because his employers are too tight to feed him.

As well as Adam, I had to employ someone new to answer the phones and help make desserts. The new waitress was Lucy, who was quiet, polite and very private school, calming irate customers in a voice like Princess Diana when Adam couldn't find their house. And within two months we were on the lookout for yet another driver as the orders just kept on piling up. Silvio, an Italian with a bushy beard, who worked days as a gardener, was the only applicant who owned a working car. So we hired him and overlooked his clothes, which were apparently made of sacking and exuded a faint aroma of potatoes.

Silvio turned out to be a good signing for the Diner. He had worked briefly as a shepherd in the Tuscan hills and would talk with misty romanticism about the bongling of sheep bells in the olive groves. More importantly, he had a keen sense of direction and never failed to sniff out a lost and lonely address.

The big, insuperable problem with deliveries is that there's no way of regulating demand. In a restaurant, once you're full, no one else can come in. But with deliveries the phone can just ring and ring and Lucy and Sophie could take order after order, and everyone expects the food in half an hour. We had a kitchen only two people could physically get into, which was fine for twenty seats in the Diner, but less so for multiple coach parties ordering from home. I wasn't complaining, exactly, it being a whole new experience to have sales on a Saturday breaking the £500 barrier for the first time. It was just that the panic and fear of being unable to cope was starting to make me gibber a little.

Imagine a typical scene. I'm bagging up an order for six, while keeping an eye on the buns for the new double order when the phone rings again. It's Adam. He thinks this is an appropriate time to tell me that maybe he wants to be a sports psychologist rather than a professional surfer. 'Great idea, Adam,' I reply absent-mindedly while cracking eggs onto the griddle one-handed and slam-dunking the shells into the bin (more expertly than Michael Jordan, I should add), 'but don't you need some sort of grounding in psychology first, maybe?'

As the next few delivery orders stack up I realise I've offended Adam and he's decided to drive very slowly. Meanwhile, Lucy is stuck with some regular customers who are taking a very long time to order. Oh no – it's the Veggies! A family of born again Christian vegetarians, these are lovely people (don't get me wrong) but they order vegetarian fry-ups that take forever to order and even longer to cook. We don't really serve breakfasts in the evening because they're too labour-intensive, but that's regulars for you: they expect you to bend the rules for them.

Some of the customers are by now waiting longer than they want for desserts and are pointedly looking over and harrumph-ing, so I quickly scan the main course orders, throw everything on the griddle and go back to help Sophie with the puddings. Three Maximum Brownies? Oh Lordy! Take three sundae glass-es. Put a little bit of chocolate brownie cake in each one, squirt of chocolate sauce, in the microwave. Dum di dum. Dum di dum. Ting! Out of the microwave, sprinkle of nuts, scoop of chocolate ice cream on each (can't get the lid off the effing vanil-la ice cream), finally, scoop of vanilla on each, then two squirts of squirty cream – squirt squirt – squirt squirt – squirt squirt – more chocolate sauce on each, then more nuts, chocolate flake, wafer, long spoon. Done!

'Chris, they didn't want nuts on those.'

'Shit and bollocks.'

Start all over again. Get as far as the squirty cream – squirt squirt – squirt squ... shhhhshhhh. Run out of cream. Dammit.

Try to scoop bit of cream off aborted puddings, avoiding nuts. Hope they don't have severe nut allergy as some may have got through. Need Adam to get more cream from Tesco's.

Then back to the burgers, now burning on the griddle. Adam, finally back to take the delivery orders, refuses to return my winning smile. 'Actually, Adam, now I think about it, you'd be a pretty good sports psychologist because you're so good at... um, sport. Nice one, go for it.' Adam happy again. Ask him to get some cream from Tesco's.

Phone rings. 'Where's my delivery order?'

'It's coming.'

'I've been waiting for 35 minutes. You said it would be 30.'

'Honestly, it's coming. The driver's just left with it.'

'I've got to go out in ten minutes.'

'I quite understand. Won't be long now. Thanks so much for your patience.'

Shuffle through delivery orders and find I haven't started cooking it yet. Bloody hell. Put it to front of rack. In the meantime all the burgers have burnt beyond use and the griddle is smoking alarmingly. Customers are looking perplexed. I chuck out the burgers and clean and restart griddle. Now, what did I do with that order...

It was impossible to keep up with it all, so we didn't try. Instead we organised a triage system. Customers eating in got priority, because they were looking at me. Next were customers picking food up, because we all know how annoying it is when you've rung up in advance and the food isn't ready when you collect it. Last were delivery customers: (a) because they're the laziest, and (b) because they can't see that you're lying to them.

Not that the lies were for lack of effort. If Adam and Silvio fell behind, and the backlog of orders stacked up, I would grab half a dozen bags and race round the houses at top speed, panting breathlessly up the drive and handing each bag of food over like

125

it was the baton in the 4 x 100m Olympic final. Then on to the next house, then the next and the next.

Pizza – or, in our case, burger – delivery is one of those jobs that people tip, even in Britain. There's no obvious reason why this should be so. It doesn't make us go any quicker or carry the food any more smoothly, which I suppose may be the historic reason for tipping taxi drivers, and we don't have time to build up any kind of rapport with the customers, as the waitresses do. Yet delivery drivers get much better tips than most restaurant staff. And they expect them, too. For a driver, a delivery without a tip is like getting a slap in the face: that split second between you giving the customer their change, and the realisation that they're closing the door, is packed with chagrin.

Even worse is when the change is 5p and the customer says, 'Keep the change,' because that implies that they're familiar with the concept of tipping but have decided not to tip you, or they think 5p is a suitable gratuity. The disgruntled delivery driver will then rummage slowly in his pockets saying, 'No, no, I've got it here somewhere, wait there,' while they say, 'Oh don't worry about that [awkward laugh], forget it,' and start to close the door. Then the driver says, 'No, I saw one here somewhere, hang on a...,' before finding that the door is closed.

126 Adam sometimes became quite unhinged with annoyance at not getting a tip, especially on cold, wet, very un-Malibu-like evenings. One night a customer rang me to complain that Adam had stood outside his door feeding the 5p change through the letterbox in 1p pieces, leaving a little pause between each coin dropping.

Seeing our success, one of the Chinese takeaways started doing deliveries – and they were showing us up by sending their man out in a bow tie, those *Art of War*-reading devils. I immediately called a Council of Drivers and Adam, Silvio and I discussed a few retaliatory options, none of which Adam was too keen on, though Silvio shrugged non-committally, perhaps not quite comprehending that I was suggesting he dressed as Elvis, or wore a cowboy hat and bandanna (since most people just referred to us as 'the American diner'). At least, I thought, we could agree that as the customer opened the door we would turn sideways on and do a 'Da-dahh!' pose, offering the food with one out-stretched hand like we were auditioning for *A Chorus Line* and saying, 'Your dinnerrrrrr, Sir/Ma'am!' Trying it out myself once or twice, though, I had to agree that it felt a little forced.

However, inspiration dawned while watching *ET The Extra-Terrestial* with Naomi's children one lazy Bank Holiday Monday. I noted how at the start of the film the pizza delivery driver goes some of the way up the drive and toots the horn, whereupon Elliot comes out of the house and goes to the car. Business is conducted through the car window, then the driver reverses the car out of the drive and shoots off. On his way back up to the house, Elliot hears a noise from the shed, drops the pizza, and the rest is film history. But, much as I enjoyed the film yet again, this time I was more impressed with the pizza delivery style. Rather than being lazy, it seemed like cool, speedy service.

So we gave it a go.

127

It was a big hit at first, and fun to do. We would be greeted by surprised smiles and big tips as we spun our wheels and shot gravel into the air on the driveways of Uckfield. Then disaster struck. I ran over a cat. It was during a late delivery to a farm-house just outside Uckfield and, as I drove into the pitch dark of the yard, I glimpsed a dozen or so furry creatures scattering in the headlights... one of them just a fraction too late. I slammed on the brakes and sat clutching the wheel, muttering, 'Oh, my God' and desperately trying to work out where the nearest vet might be.

Alas, there was no need for a vet, though the poor thing looked quite peaceful, considering. I placed it beside me at the door while I rang the bell and then wondered awkwardly what I was supposed to do with the cartons containing Big Max and chips(for three). Did I deliver them anyway? And what about the money: should I waive the charge or offer a discount? Clearly there are moments that no operational manual or business guru can prepare you for. And in case I was tempted to flee, the security lights at last flicked on, bathing me, the deceased cat and the takeaway cartons in a fierce glow like some macabre son et lumière. A lanky teenager opened the door. 'Yeah, cool, man! burgers!' he exclaimed, reaching out a hand, the whiff of ganja wafting out from behind him onto the porch. There was a pause while we both looked at the cat and I began my explanation. 'Ah, that's terrible, man, but hey have they all got coleslaw? Yesss! And extra gherkins!' Then, clutching the bags to his chest, he handed over a twenty-pound-note and pushed the door shut. Only food can talk to a man in the grip of the munchies.

The next day, still wracked with guilt, I drove back to the house only to be met by a brand new notice at the gate reading 'Deliveries, please park here.' Apparently the au pair and his friends were supposed to have kept the gate shut or warned me about the kittens on the loose. 'It's the third we've lost this week,' the owner lamented as she poured me a forgiving cup of tea.

It was time to go back to parking on the road.

Delivering food ought to be rather a good job for an employee. Your manager's not watching, so you can smoke, you can go at whatever pace you fancy, you can stop off in a layby and read a book, you can take a friend with you, or a dog (though that's not recommended), you can provide your own musical soundtrack or enjoy listening to a talking book, you can conserve brain cells by using none whatsoever during the course of your shift, you can chat to people on your mobile phone while driving. Then, when you're not delivering you can lean on a counter and flirt with the female staff in the shop, very much to the annoyance of the manager. For this you get tips, you get payment per delivery, all on top of basic wages that have to be above the national minimum. So, the question arises: why does nobody want to do the bloody job?

The inherent structural problem with delivery of food is that the only people who are willing to do it are the ones least likely to have a reliable car. Thus, on top of all the other problems of the caterer is added the worry of having to predict car problems; every wet and windy night becomes especially tense. On the plus side, on the few rainy nights when Silvio's car would start, we were treated to the sight of him in a special home-made hat made of a hessian-like material – a cross between a monk's cowl, a tam-o'-shanter, and the sort of hat you make from folded newspaper. But now every little traffic problem became a mini-nightmare. Every hole in the road, every failed traffic light, every gas main repair, meant that our customers got cold food.

As takings went up on deliveries, so we had more people coming in to the restaurant to eat as well. Perhaps they had been too nervous to try a new place at first, but the temptation of getting a giant burger and a tub of Häagen-Dazs delivered right to their settee in front of their telly had proved too much. Then, having got over that first barrier, they felt they could risk coming in.

There was something about doing deliveries to people's houses that made everything seem friendlier, too. Incidents of violent disorder dropped off dramatically as I grew to be on nodding terms with Gary A's mum, and on stroking terms with Gary B's bulldog. Gary C predictably made a hoax delivery call, but blew his cover by ordering it to his next-door neighbour's house and then standing grinning by his front gate, giving me the excuse to ban him once and for all.

There weren't as many hoax calls as I'd expected, though the occasional person did seem to think that by ordering food to the house of someone they had a grudge against, that enemy/ex-lover/former boss would be made to pay. You can never make anyone pay for anything if they don't want to, especially if they haven't ordered it, so it's only the business that suffers. Gary B's sister, Lisa, claimed that we'd delivered an 'off' burger to her and demanded a refund. After I patiently explained the physical impossibility of the burger being off, she said that was fine, told me to forget about the refund, and we parted on perfectly cordial terms. Then the next evening she ordered more food, and when Adam got to the house calmly said she'd changed her mind after all and didn't want it. Clever, really.

It doesn't take any special psychological skill to spot a hoax call, mainly because they tend to be delivered in a little juvenile voice with giggling in the background. If they get past that barrier they often fall down on the supplementary question such as 'What's your postcode?' or 'You're lying, aren't you?' and quickly hang up. Hoaxers also tend to order wildly extravagantly and add silly, improbable toppings – though you shouldn't jump to conclusions and start hurling abuse as so do pregnant women.

Talking of which, Dani and Scott (the post-pub lovely couple) had got pregnant and moved in together – one of those little details I wouldn't have known until we started delivering and could see the customer in their own environment. The evidence of feminine influence was unequivocal: no more late-night orders for triple burgers to the accompaniment of drunken yelling in the background ('Eh Scott, ask 'er for a furburger, mate. Huh huh.') Now Scott was ordering a more modest, two-person portion, maybe with a side salad and a Diet Coke, more in keeping with his position as expectant father.

Dani came into the shop one afternoon with Scott and shared a Burger'n'Hash Combo with him. Something was up, though. They seemed tense. As a general rule when I detect a problem, I never ask if anything's wrong with the food. Managers are supposed to, so you can remedy the problem straight away rather than have customers just go elsewhere without you knowing why, but criticism is embarrassing, so when I sense a problem I prefer to hide until the waitress tells me they've gone.

However, it turned out that it was nothing to do with the meal. Dani had just started her contractions and to Scott's fury was insisting on getting some proper food before going to hospital, carbing up, as she called it. Not only that, but she had first got off with Scott on the way home from the Diner, so it held a special place in their hearts.

And all went well. They proudly brought the baby in to show us on the way home from hospital and Dani suggested we offered a special discount for women who were breastfeeding. A nice idea, but once again I couldn't quite see how to word it.

Jamboree!

THERE'S A FEELING THAT OVERWHELMS YOU when you discover that your business is becoming reliably profitable – a rush of self-esteem that feels a lot like being in love. For days I wandered about with a ridiculous grin that I couldn't wipe off my face, or found myself juggling salad vegetables, even gave a resounding 'Amen' to one of Miss Green's upbeat homilies over the bread and tea. The staff soon cottoned on to my new mood and inundated me with requests for pay rises.

132   Then Adam suggested that we had a celebration, some sort of staff outing. He had been hankering for an office party ever since Lucy had joined the team and he was in no mood to wait for Christmas. Instead, he reckoned we should close the Diner for a day and all go surfing off Brighton beach, and then maybe have a barbecue and play cool games like the one he had played on a Club 18–30 holiday, where you put a banana down the bikin—
'No! NO! NO!' was the loud and unanimous reply.

The idea, however, of a collective day/night out seemed to stick. 'What about clubbing?' asked Sophie brightly.

'You want to go clubbing, with me and Silvio, and Adam?' I asked in return.

Sophie shuddered. 'Actually, fair point, scrub that.'

Then Silvio suggested a day out in the countryside, picnicking, getting drunk and just generally communing with nature. After initially being a bit wary of his wild hair and whiff of root vegetables, the female staff had rather taken to Silvio; they liked his Italian accent and laidback manner, so different to Adam's boyish enthusiasm. Plus he exuded a certain sort of competence – he was good at getting food to its destination on time, leaving them with fewer ruffled feathers to smooth amongst customers.

'Yes, a picnic. Let's have a picnic!' chorused Lucy, Sophie and Catherine, with a quieter echo from Adam. But not just a picnic: being the very profitable, rather marvellous Maximum Diner, we needed to push the boat out (literally, as it happened) with a Summer Jamboree!

I've not been a big fan of workplace parties since having to endure, as manager of a chain restaurant, motivational 'hype sessions' (or 'gripe sessions', as we called them) to foster team spirit. Inevitably pent-up antagonisms would get released under the influence of alcohol, and bitter rows, fisticuffs even, would ensue. But our Maximum Diner outing would clearly be different – an established team celebrating an upturn in trade. Also I felt it would be wrong to quietly shelve the plan. Like most British people, I'm good at stoically suffering the bad times but rotten at properly celebrating the good ones. Personally, I blame Kipling for all that 'if you can meet with Triumph and Disaster and treat those two imposters just the same' nonsense.

133

Adam was anyway stepping up the pressure by reminding me, daily, how excited everyone was about the idea. From Lucy, Sophie and Catherine's blank looks and careful avoidance of the subject, you could have fooled me, but the Jamboree somehow gathered momentum, a date was set, and a concept (as it were) established. We were to have twelve hours of fun and debauchery, the kind of day the young Ernest Hemingway might have enjoyed with his mates. It would be pleasure heaped on pleasure: a pub here, a boating session there, a picnic tea, another pub, a movie, followed by maybe another meal and another few drinks, before going home drunk but happy in the small hours.

The day was scheduled to begin with a late breakfast of coffee and croissant at the Diner. A very late breakfast, in fact, as Sophie had made a last-ditch effort the night before to avoid coming, claiming a doctor's appointment. But she hadn't done her homework properly and when I asked what time the appointment was, she said, 'Oh about eleven, I think.' 'Great!' piped up Adam. 'We'll wait for you.'

Sophie arrived looking thoroughly bad tempered about the whole thing, but then, I reasoned, she's never really been a morning person anyway; she's probably hung over. Hemingway was probably the same. She sat morosely in a corner with Catherine, studiously avoiding eye contact with Adam, or John, the friendly, polite and immaculately turned-out sixth-former he'd brought with him. John was a star of the school's drama group, and exactly the kind of person mothers like their sons and daughters to invite home. In fact, he should have a great future presenting children's television, if he ever gets over the shock of Our Terrible Day Out.

Thankfully, at this point he and Adam still seemed enthusiastic, as did Lucy, who had arrived with a hip flask that she was well on her way to finishing. John kept trying to engage her in conversation, but was wasting her time, because, lovely though

134

Lucy is, she just doesn't really do conversation. Looking pretty in jodhpurs and hacking jacket? Certainly. Light banter and witty exchanges? Not really.

We sat in silence waiting for Silvio, punctuated by occasional attempts from me to break the ice. 'Another croissant? Anyone?' No answer. 'Another croissant, John?' 'No thanks, Chris, I'm stuffed!' Pause. 'Another croissant, Lucy?' Shake of the head. 'Another croissant, Catheri—?' 'NO! No one wants another croissant, Chris.' This from Catherine, testily.

Eventually I rang up Silvio, and he said he'd decided not to come, since he'd seen lots of countryside before, what with being a shepherd and all. Then, with my back to the others, I phoned Naomi to see if she'd step into the breach, but she was clinging to her alibi of helping out at school. 'Fine,' I said tersely, momentarily downcast, but the sight of the taxis pulling up served to stiffen my resolve, and a few minutes later we were wending our way through country lanes towards our first pub of the day.

The Anchor is a few miles from Uckfield, set beside the Ouse, downriver from where the Uck flows into it. The pub is popular locally for hiring out boats, and the idea was to start our day out in the country by going boating, then to have a pub lunch and spend most of the afternoon drinking. The evening was still an open book; we would see how the spirits took us.

135

The weather wasn't helping those spirits, though. It was one of those murky summer days when you think the mist is going to rise and everything will turn out fantastic, but it doesn't – it just stays dull all day and you consider emigrating. From the point of view of selling burgers, these kind of days are fantastic, hot days being terrible for business as too many people have barbecues. But for a day on the river, sunny weather is kind of *de rigueur*.

As, too, are boats. What we all imagined we were going to be sailing up the Ouse on I don't know. A cabin cruiser? A yacht? A three-masted clipper with a crew dressed all in white to pipe us aboard? Whatever, there was a collective scowl of disappointment at the Anchor's selection of dirty, bashed-up canoes. In fact, 'canoes' doesn't really do them justice, as canoes have a certain Hiawatha-style appeal, whereas Hiawatha wouldn't have been seen dead in one of these slimy, plastic buckets.

Still, we were committed, and while Adam was carefully trying to organise us into boy girl, boy girl, boy girl, Catherine and Sophie got into a boat together and paddled away into the mist. The rest of us turned to help a swaying Lucy safely into a canoe, which we did, eventually. Then Adam quickly leapt into the boat with her and pushed off, leaving John and I to pair up.

John was clearly annoyed to find himself sitting in a canoe with me rather than Lucy, but on the bright side we could at least paddle in sync and we set off after Catherine and Sophie at a cracking pace, leaving Adam and Lucy in our wake, bashing helplessly into the riverbank and continually having to retrieve Lucy's oar from where she dropped it in the water while trying to fend off swans.

We caught up with the lead boat easily enough, but then none of us were sure what to do next. I had assumed the day would gather a momentum of its own, but it seemed becalmed as we tried to make small talk about reeds, types of trees and the various waterhopping insects buzzing around us. I found my attempts to be the life and soul of the party floundering.

'Lunchtime!' I exclaimed. 'We'll race you back, and whoever loses buys the first round.'

'We didn't bring any money. You said it was all on the Diner.'

'Well, race you back anyway.'

After a couple of paddles I realised that we had left Catherine and Sophie behind, going around in circles. Never mind: we soon came across Adam and Lucy, who had only got about thirty yards from the pub before they decided to stop paddling and have a water fight, from inside the same boat.

It was definitely time for a drink, and so we dumped the canoes and went into the pub – or squelched in, in the case of Lucy and Adam – and I started giving the drinks orders.

'Have they got ID?' said the barman.

'It's okay,' I said, 'we're all eating, and they're over sixteen.'

'They have to be eighteen, and they need ID,' said the barman, looking at Lucy. She had taken off her trousers and hung them over the back of her chair, and was sitting steaming drunkenly in her knickers.

'No, but we're all eating, and they're with an adult, so legally they only have to be sixteen,' I reasoned, reasonably.

'Not round here they don't. Will you put your trousers on love? You have to be eighteen.'

'But according to the licensing laws...'

'I'm not arguing.'

As we settled down with our Cokes and orange juices, Catherine and Sophie walked in.

'He won't let us drink,' John told them.

'And he's making Lucy put her trousers on,' said Adam, holding Lucy's arm to steady her as she set about the tricky task of pulling cold wet jeans over damp thighs.

It was the day's new low point. We sat in a circle silently eating ploughman's lunches, Lucy shivering, despite the diminishing hip flask, with nobody daring to utter a word. Actually, to be fair, it wasn't easy to talk. Anything that was said was said to the whole, miserable group, which put intolerable pressure on whoever was holding the floor to come up with something witty or interesting. If only we could have got some sub-conversations going, a murmur of chitchat would have made everyone feel less like they were making a presentation to the whole group, but

137

each time we got close the conversations all stopped at the same time, plunging us back again into silence.

By this stage, we were all starting to shiver a bit, too, so I brought the Frisbee out and suggested chucking it about in the fields by the river to keep us warm. We trooped out of the pub, went in the field, chucked it up a tree, couldn't get it down and so trooped back into the pub again.

The day was rapidly taking on a kind of legendary crapness, which might have evoked a Dunkirk spirit, but didn't, as we wordlessly waited for our taxis to arrive. It really required someone to have the courage to say, 'Look, this is terrible, let's go home,' but the only person in a position to do that was me... and I kept thinking that something this bad had to get better. It was only mid-afternoon, and we were supposed to have a full day and evening of entertainment ahead of us.

I gave Catherine the money for one taxi and got in the other with Adam and Lucy. The taxi driver looked a bit dubious about her trousers, but they were starting to dry out a bit, so he let it go. As we neared the Diner, however, the prospect of trying to drum up any more enthusiasm was too painful to contemplate. 'Just here is fine, thanks,' I said to the driver and got out, shoving a twenty-pound note through the window. 'Take these two wherever they want to go.'

I could see Adam and Lucy looking at me through the back window of the taxi as it drove off and I left them to it, and walked home in the gathering dusk to get drunk with Naomi.

The following few days at work were a little tense, with everyone a bit tetchy and guilt-ridden. The only person who had happy memories of the day was Adam, though you couldn't help but notice that a slight awkwardness had appeared between him and

Lucy where none had existed before. Gradually, though, the dust began to settle on the first and last staff party, the strained atmosphere dissipated and the staff went back to chatting happily again, much to the annoyance of the customers, who had an increasingly hard job getting themselves noticed.

'What did you expect, Chris?' Naomi had asked on the evening of the debacle. 'They're teenagers first, colleagues second – you know that.' She was right, of course, and in a sense had got straight to the heart of the problem. I was spending far too much of my time surrounded by people I didn't really identify with: people who were either too young, or too violent, or too busy eating their lunch. It was then, before the moment of insight had faded, that I proposed, which surprised me as I hadn't meant to propose at all. I waited. Naomi went quiet for a moment and then began to explain, clearly and quite sweetly, why marriage might not work for us.

I could outline here a list of the reasons she gave; I could tell you about the access battles she was locked in with her ex-husband or the stresses of my having to work even longer hours at the Diner, but none of those were really the issue. What mattered was that Naomi knew for certain that her days of pregnancy and baby-rearing were over. And she didn't want to marry someone who might try and persuade her a few years down the line to have another couple of kids just for his sake.

This wasn't, of course, the first time we had touched on the subject, but it was the first time we'd done so without agreeing that we couldn't know what the future would hold or that we should see how it goes. Instead, I had to face up to the idea that we were good friends and lovers but that was probably the best it would get.

At least that's what I understood in hindsight. At the time I just thought, Oh bollocks, I'm really going to have to throw myself into the business now.

Which was not at all what I wanted to do. Having at last reached a position of financial safety I would have been happy to enjoy myself rather than strive for dizzy new heights of wealth and success. Perhaps I'm just not competitive enough for the cut and thrust of empire building – as a child, for instance, I was always quite content to lose in games of football or Monopoly, so long as it kept my three stroppier and older siblings happy. And I've heard it said that the difference between the British and Americans is that, when they've each made a million, the Brit retires to a big house in the country and takes up fishing while the American sees it as the promising first step toward making the billion. I believe the point is meant to be pejorative against the lazy Brits, but really, who needs a billion of anything?

Not that a billion was the issue exactly. I still owed money on the Diner, although the debt was at last whittling down. But clearly it was time to discover what my true ambitions were – both for the restaurant and for myself, and to do that I would need to claw back a bit of space from work.

So I made Catherine assistant manager. I don't know why I hadn't thought of her before. Though just eighteen, and still at school, Catherine had a maturity, sense of responsibility and downright efficiency that was amazing in one so young – and in a girl who drank so much. I would see her staggering off, half carried by her friends at closing time on a Saturday night, but at ten the next morning she'd come bouncing into work with a cheery hello, whip on an apron and have got me a coffee and be chopping onions before you could say, 'Urrhh, can you draw those blinds, please?' She never wanted to stop for a break, was never ill, and never complained about anything (apart from the staff party, which is fair enough).

The Diner was in good hands. Now for the planning.

140

Elvis comes to town

UP UNTIL OUR ARRIVAL, the spiritual heart of Uckfield was more or less the end of aisle three in Tesco's, equidistant from the bananas, the ten-items-or-less checkout and the newspaper racks. That had become the equivalent of the old parish pump: the place you'd stop and shoot the breeze with old friends or, in my case, duck behind a large merchandising stand to avoid bumping into someone or other I had banned from the Diner. Some people, of course, disagreed, arguing that the town's geographical and philosophical centre could be placed firmly out-side Curry's on the High Street, or at least on the thirty-yard stretch of pavement that goes from Superdrug in the south to Sussex Stationers in the north. Some even claimed the centre as the rack of old shoes in the third charity shop up the High Street on the left. My new mission, I decided, was to change that, to breathe fresh life into the top of the High Street and to make the Diner the beating heart of this town.

Now, that would be something worth fighting for, better than mere riches (though they would be quite nice, too). The Maximum Diner and I could make a real difference to the town. We could be Big in Uckfield.

So, taking a closer view I tried to think of local events that brought people together and gave them a sense of community – because that was where we would focus our promotional efforts. There was only one that really mattered, and that was Carnival. We would seize the moment and enter a float in the procession.

There are people in Uckfield who write off its Carnival as boring and 'the same every year' – which rather misses the point that that's supposed to be the point of it. Personally I look forward to the occasion. It's held on the first Saturday of September every year, when the nights are still warm and there's a bit of holiday spirit left, and, no matter how bored they claim to be, everybody turns out. The buzz in the town is palpable from the moment, a week before, when the Funfair arrives in town. I love to watch the fair vehicles slowly rolling down the High Street, as they must have done for centuries, with the rides all folded up before being assembled on Luxford Field, the dog-shitty sloping football pitch that passes for a civic amenity in Uckfield.

Carnival Day itself starts a little unpromisingly, with a children's costume procession, when a straggle of kids arrayed in odd assortments of cloth, cardboard and face paint walk down the High Street, eliciting gasps of wonder from shoppers as they stop, point and ask, 'What the hell is that one supposed to be?' By the early evening the crowds are starting to gather allowing plenty of time for the roving bands of fourteen- to twenty-five-year-olds to get nicely pissed and lairy before the flare goes up at 8.30pm, signalling the start of the main procession.

142

We British don't really know how to react to a procession. Most people (and I include myself) tend to adopt a fixed grin that's meant to convey, 'I'm really enjoying this. It's so lovely to see ancient traditions carrying on, and no, I'm not ogling the majorettes. I won't whoop and holler, thank you very much, but I will reward the best floats with a little light applause and I may give a discreet wave at the small children riding on them (but only if they wave first).'

Of course, the more drunk you get the more appreciation you might show, but there's no getting away from the fact that you're watching a flatbed lorry carrying the Junior Rugby Club or Friends of the Rotarians, enthusiastically waving bits of wire and papier-mâché at you. It's just not Rio.

I reckoned, however, that a Maximum Diner float could break through such mediocrity and add real all-American pizzazz to the procession, as well as provide a nice bit of advertising. And I knew just how I was going to do it. I would present to the people of Uckfield, for the first time... Elvis Presley (Vegas period) gliding down the High Street in his white sparkly cowboy-style jumpsuit, belting out his hits to an audience so stunned they drop their crappy van-bought burgers in the gutter.

I rang a cockney agent in *The Stage,* who promised me that for 'half a monkey' I'd get an Elvis, that was 'the bollocks'. Maybe I misheard and he said 'utter bollocks', but his spiel sounded too good to miss, and I made the booking straight away. I'd left it too late to organise a flatbed lorry but I borrowed my brother-in-law's Second World War, open-topped Willy's Jeep, which looks beautiful and has a nice throaty roar, while I dressed myself up as General Patton (not very festive, perhaps, but it went well with the Jeep and I already had the helmet).

The agent had told me that Elvis would bring his own sound system, which sounded quite impressive, until Terry (as my Elvis was called at home) turned up with a smallish ghetto-blaster and

143

a selection of pre-recorded tapes of himself performing Elvis classics. These he intended to mime to, which seemed an odd decision. If he had to mime, then surely it would be better to mime to the King himself singing Elvis classics. But no, Terry was adamant.

There was also the problem that Terry didn't really look much like Elvis, even in a passably decent Vegas suit, which prompted me to ask what precisely the two hundred and fifty quid I was forking out was for. This stumped him, too, his normal charge being much lower, but time was pressing and we had a show to get on the road. And there our problems began, as Terry point-blank refused to stand up in the back of the Jeep, which he said was dangerous, despite my protestations that young men had driven past sniper fire in this very Jeep, and miming with your seatbelt on was just not rock'n'roll.

To get a decent place in the procession we had to wait for three hours in line before it all started. So, for two and three-quarter hours I sat with Elvis-Terry sulking in the passenger seat beside me, while passing youths mocked us both. Then I noticed that I hadn't written 'Maximum Diner' anywhere on the Jeep, so I tried to cut out letters from coloured paper and stick them on the side. It looked horribly botched, and worse was to come. As we set off down the hill, towards the crowds of 15,000 or so Uckfield citizenry, Elvis got major stage fright and threatened to desert, especially when the crowd started chucking coins, an Uckfield Carnival tradition I had forgotten to mention to him.

Looking in the rear-view mirror I could see he had abandoned all attempts at mime and was simply cowering in the back like a white, sparkling jelly. That provoked the crowd even more, and I was glad I had the foresight to wear a tin helmet. For my part, I'd brought along some distress flares (rather suitably) and set them off at intervals, to the further consternation of Elvis, who moaned that they'd mark his suit.

At the very end of the procession the electrics went on the Jeep, sending sparks shooting out from the foot pedals whenever I pressed them, and I had to get it towed to a garage.

The whole sorry Carnival episode had cost me hours of effort and hassle, at least a 'monkey', and maybe a 'carpet' and a 'pony' on top. Plus I had looked a complete knob. In the weeks to come I tried to make out that he was meant to be a crap, ironic Elvis, but the moral of the story is not to be snotty about other people's efforts at Carnival until you've tried it yourself.

As might be expected, there was no dramatic increase in sales following Carnival. We were getting more than two 'bags' a week (bags o' sand = grand; okay, I'll stop that now), which was a decent enough turnover. But we were also spending a lot on employing extra drivers, so the money didn't really translate into profit. Added to this was our failure in pressing home the message that we were right at the heart of town life, its pacemaker if you like. We needed to get back to the drawing board and work out a marketing strategy that combined increased sales with more of a message about who we were.

To that end, I conducted a series of informal focus groups amongst the staff and regular customers, asking such questions as: If the Maximum Diner were a dog, what sort of dog would it be? I hadn't second-guessed what answers I was looking for, but 'small yappy thing' was probably not it (thank you, Adam). The canine qualities I hoped we exhibited would be playfulness, loyalty, willingness to leap into a stream or chase a stick, not snapping at people, but not being one of those pain-in-the-neck dogs that always roll on their backs wanting their tummy tickled. What did that make us? Labrador? Retriever? So, focus groups – not as easy as they appear.

145

In fact it turned out that our reputation for post-pub violence and being a hangout for local yobs was putting us squarely in the category of lovable Rottweiler – the sort of dog that no matter how much you reassure people is safe, most just don't want to get too close to. Being such a small place exacerbated the problem, for if any trouble did kick off it was difficult to get out of the way. And, even without the yobs, our size was an issue. You could all too easily hear what was happening on any other table, whether that was a couple of teenagers nervously struggling through their first date or Robbo and Gary A marvelling in their own blunt way about the breasts on a girl on the next table. Often I had to turn the music up to high volume to prevent a family overhearing what was being said about the daughter/mother, or to cover the embarrassment of some poor parent whose child was screaming.

One of the benefits of taking a young family to a place like, say, McDonald's which is big enough to absorb noise, is that if children misbehave no one really cares. In the Diner, by contrast, parents with difficult children were having their parenting skills judged by the rest of the customers. And, anyway, what sort of influence would those children be subjected to? Many years ago I went into a Boston diner and the customers all sat at long tables, encouraged to talk to the stranger next to them. I had hoped to create a little of that atmosphere at the Maximum Diner, by virtue of its very smallness, but the crucial difference was that, in Boston, positioned just outside the gates of Harvard, you might end up talking to a Nobel laureate or future president, whereas here you were more likely to be sitting perilously close to Guppy as he struggled to stay upright after a lunchtime of strong cider and crack.

What we needed were more seats, spread out in a bigger area. This would mean knocking down some walls and building an extension to the seating area, and perhaps also repositioning the kitchen. Our kitchen was out the back, whereas classic American diners have an open-plan kitchen behind a counter, so that customers had the option of sliding into a booth or sitting along the counter on a high stool, where they could chat to the staff and watch their food being cooked. I wasn't too thrilled about having customers looking at me cooking, as I get a bit stressed when we're busy (and when I'm really stressed I start kicking things). So we worked out a remodelling of the room which transformed the old kitchen into restaurant seating, and had the kitchen behind a counter – but no seats alongside it. This was a dream solution. It meant the Diner would have two more booths (eight extra covers that could make a big difference), but keep its cosy feel, and in the kitchen I would be on show but still get to kick stuff around in relative privacy.

The only real problem with the prototype Maximum Diner II was that there would be no longer any physical barrier between the kitchen and the yobs. The kitchen would, literally, be in the firing line – and with the added bonus that yobs would be able to lean over the counter and steal the food as it was being cooked.

This was a very real worry, as by now a new generation of yobs were flexing their muscles and having a go, and – guess what? – they were led by Gary D. (Okay, his name wasn't actually Gary but he did seem a natural heir to the title.) 'Gary D' was even more dangerous than Garys A, B and C. Most of the time he stayed at home under curfew with an electronic tag on his leg, but every now and then the authorities had to let him loose to see if he was still dangerous. Then he'd go on a bit of a spree, beat a few people up – on one memorable occasion with a paving slab – before being arrested again. He only got into trouble for about one incident in five, because most people were too frightened to complain. Even the man who got hit with the paving slab decided to let bygones be bygones.

Still, even the dimmest, nastiest hooligan (which pretty much defined Gary D) recognises that attacking owners of licensed premises is a bad idea, as it can get you banned from pubs. So he rarely gave me trouble, except one Christmas when he knocked my crib about, broke the head off a Wise Man, then abused and threw Coke over a fellow diner who had had the temerity to wear make-up whilst being a man. 'You're banned,' I shouted, while the police car drew up, which felt good to say, but wasn't quite the whole story. I mean, how precisely was I going to manage to throw him out when he next lurched into the Diner tanked up on fifteen pints of lager and demanded a burger?

I'd just have to close the Diner before he got there. It was the excuse I was looking for to close at 10.30 anyway. Sure, I could still have done with the post-pub income, especially with the refurbishment costs. But the Diner was moving into a whole new era of being a proper restaurant, and violent drunks were no longer going to feature in our customer profile.

So we had our last ever late-night Friday, a joyous, emotional occasion with one of the town's junkies, an old mate of Guppy's, calling me a cunt over and over again for no apparent reason. The following week we put the shutters down and escaped, pushing our way through the gathering crowds in a scene reminiscent of the the US Embassy evacuation, Saigon, 1975.

148   I didn't know what to do with myself I had so much free time. Home in time for *Newsnight* – the luxury! During building work I enjoyed my first holiday for four years and came back for the grand reopening of our new, proper restaurant. The first Saturday we took over £1000 in one day for the first time ever, and we still made last orders in the pub.

Bigging it up

I DIDN'T LET THE NEW SOLVENCY GO TO MY HEAD. In a lecture at Leeds Polytechnic we'd been given a Top Ten list of business advice and, though I've forgotten the other nine, I do remember that one of them was to 'Beware the good times'. I always thought it rather mean-spirited advice, even though at the time its practical application was being driven home to me every Saturday of the football season.

For the year I went to college, my team, Brighton and Hove Albion, were in the First Division (now the Premier League) and in the final of the FA Cup. Living Up North I only got to see away games, but over the following three years I saw Brighton lose in just about every stadium in the north of England as we slipped down and further down the divisions until they/we were bottom of the bottom division, only goal difference away from being dropped from the league altogether. I never saw Brighton win. In Barnsley we lost two-nil and I had the added delight of missing the first half (wrong bus), being chased round the stadium by Barnsley yobs, and being assaulted by a police officer. Eventually our own Goldstone Ground was sold off as a retail park to pay debts and we (I say 'we' though, like most of the Brighton support, I'd by now lost heart) had to hire a stadium to play our home games.

The rot had set in during those good times, when the directors had embarked on such a collective bender that when they sobered up it had all gone – literally gone – even the stadium. Brighton had made the mistake of thinking it was a big club when it was obvious to anyone that we were just a little club that had got lucky for a season and should spend accordingly.

We weren't going to make that mistake at the Diner: we were a little place, making a small profit, and grateful for it. The bank had been paid off, my brother's debt was diminishing, albeit at a fairly sluggish rate, while on a personal level I remained frugal; the notion of forsaking all wordly pleasures until clear of every debt and a free man struck me as rather romantic.

But I discovered after a few months that it's not as much fun as it sounds. So, in a rash weekend, I bought a racehorse and a nice big car.

To be fair, Beau was actually an ex-racehorse – with a limp and a personality disorder – and I didn't really buy her so much as get blackmailed into rescuing her for the cost of upkeep and transport, before she got sent to the knacker's yard.

An Irish throroughbred, Beau was a beauty and she seemed to take to me from the start, trotting over and whinnying, then nuzzling me in a way that left a warm feeling and a coat covered in chestnut horsehair. I installed her in a DIY livery yard, which meant that the farmer provided the stables and fields but I was left to do all the feeding, mucking out and general looking after the horse myself. At the stables, I soon became introduced to the strange world of amateur horsewomen – all the owners, apart from me, were women – many of whom appeared to be a couple of bales short of a haystack (possibly the result of falling off a horse and being kicked in the head once or twice too often). The trick to acceptance in this world, I soon discovered, was to be as bossy as possible to other people, while completely besotted with the horses. Think Princess Anne – but more so.

As a teenage hunt saboteur, my mission had been to bate people like this to the point where they actually tried to horsewhip me, partly for fun and partly to divert their attention away from the fox/stag. But there's a silent camaraderie that exists between people who haul themselves out of bed when it's still dark outside, don green wellies and go and stand in a patch of mud waiting for a horse to finish its oats and go cantering around dewy fields. I found that, once you had melted the glacial exterior, these women could be rather nice. Mad and muddy, but nice.

The cantering, however, was a bit of a problem. I'd been taken riding as a child, by my older sister, so I felt I knew a thing or two about horses. But not horses like this: fast horses, bred for speed rather than brains. It soon became clear why Beau had been destined for the knacker's yard, as when she wasn't allowed to gallop she became incensed, leaping about like a bucking bronco. I solved this problem by always letting her get her own way, but even I could see that this was only storing up trouble for later.

Thank God for cars, then; faithful cars that do what you want, when you want. I justified the expenditure on a large four-by-four by claiming that the lease finance would come out of the advertising budget since it had a wheel cover on the back that could be used to carry the Maximum Diner logo. Besides, I had a horse now and was part of the country set, so who knew

151

when I might be called upon to rescue something or other from a ditch?

The reason I was able to ease off for a bit, apart from having some disposable income for the first time in five years, was that I had finally found a replacement daytime supervisor to work opposite shifts to Catherine. Her name was Liz and she was a regular customer, along with her teenage daughters.

Normally, I dislike employing customers; it's a sure way to lose regulars, while the new staff member soon discovers that life is nowhere near as much fun on the other side of the counter. But employing Liz turned out to be the best personnel choice I'd made since Catherine. She was warm, kind, understanding, fun, loyal, and Irish. In temperament she could be the love child of Graham Norton and *EastEnders*' Pat Butcher, unlikely though that union is. With her arrival the Diner began to attract a whole new side of Uckfield society, from the town's gay men (a persecuted minority given the yobocracy that governed during the hours of darkness), to one of the town's part-time prostitutes (or escorts, as she liked to put it), and, for some reason, a succession of women who came in to tell Liz tearfully that they were thinking of leaving their husbands.

These were the glory days of the Maximum Diner. Over the following months it felt like I was presiding over a small town café-Camelot. We got busier and busier, we had wonderful, beautiful staff, a mixed and much more interesting clientele, and the best fast food menu in town. Our delivery service was booming, too, and it wouldn't be pushing things too far to claim that our riders were replacing the milkman or the pools collector of old as the community or (let's be honest) gossip nexus of the town. Since the job of milkman has been destroyed by cheap milk being sold

152

as a loss leader by supermarkets, perhaps it was time restaurant delivery people stepped into the role, checking on old folk, looking out for mischief, sleeping with saucy housewives, etc. I know that Adam was keen to help out with at least one of these roles because he kept on telling me so.

I wasn't swimming in cash, but I had been proved right about the diner concept – it really could become the hub of the town – and I believed I was onto a winner at last. But I should have known that in a very small-scale firm, as soon as you get a nice team together, making a healthy profit, someone is bound to get pregnant, or arrested, or go to university. In one memorable week, the Diner managed to score two out of three. Catherine was offered a place at university and, although she was happy to stay on for the few months until term began it was clear that she had begun an entirely new and divergent career path; one that could take her, if her talents were properly appreciated, way beyond the Fast Food Industry, all the way to becoming Head of General Motors, Chairman of the Joint Chiefs of Staff and President of Europe, if such a joint post existed. There are few things for a manager so upsetting as the imminent departure of a wonderful member of staff, and I dreaded the prospect of there being no one to come rushing in to help when a coach party turned up unexpectedly, or defuse a looming yob catastrophe with charm and tact and blackmail.

Then Sophie announced she was pregnant and about to leave us. At the time single parents were being victimised as lazy, feck- less, immoral housing-queue jumpers. The ones that I knew couldn't have been less like that. Naomi and most of her single parent friends were desperate to work, as the only route to regaining the self-respect and financial security that had been denied them by divorce and life on social security. Rather than feckless, they were, if anything, overly feckful. Sophie, on the other hand, was cheerfully unfazed by all the negative stereotypes of the pregnant teenager and gave in her notice within weeks of testing positive. When Adam, unable to hide his fury at someone else getting his lusty way with her, tried to deflate her with stories of the rotten life she would lead in Highfield Court, the block of flats reserved for the single and desperate (good customers of ours, incidentally, so not entirely desperate), Sophie hardly heard him. Happier than ever, she threw herself into pregnancy with the same enthusiasm she'd had for interrogating customers about their taste in clothes.

Their replacements were two of Liz's daughters: Sally, the same age as Catherine, and Laura, who at just sixteen became our new youngest member of staff. Like Sense and Sensibility, they were opposites in personality. Sally was reserved, prudent and calm, always cheerful but you wouldn't know it unless you got talking. Laura was bouncy, tactile and effervescent, and very popular with the younger office crowd. Despite being three women from the same family, they all got on well together, chatting, supporting and teasing each other good-naturedly and, even better, the two girls proved adept at covering up for their mum's more chaotic approach to cooking.

Meanwhile, Dani and Scott were coming in with the new baby, taking advantage of our impressive baby-changing facility and non-smoking area. I would have liked to have banned smoking altogether, but coming on top of the new early closing I felt a smoking ban could drive the yobs out altogether, just when we were enjoying their company (and money) for breakfast, all meek and well behaved. The baby-changing facility was a collapsible white shelf, kept spotlessly clean and provided with a range of wet wipes, etc – a facility that became popular amongst the young folks as somewhere private, clean and flat to snort cocaine off, which explained why they had got so chatty. Reluctantly I had to tighten up on toilet use by non-customers, and on stressful shifts avoid any temptation to lick the shelf.

In general, things were going well, turnover was up and everything seemed to be humming along in a manner I'd not have dreamt of a year or two earlier. Yet the trumpeted advantages of entrepreneurial success still eluded me. Instead of being my own boss I seemed to be at the mercy of everyone else, particularly with regard to illness, and as I was staffing up there was more likelihood of people ringing in sick, their cars breaking down, their children getting ill, their houses burning down and so on.

Employees are only expected to act as employees, and I used to do so myself when I was a chain manager: if half the staff rang in sick, but it was my night off and I had something planned, that was too bad, we'd just have to offer rubbish service. But in your own restaurant you can't get away with such an attitude; you have a duty of responsibility to make sure your customers have a wonderful time whatever the cost to you and your sorry excuse for a life. Having said that, I doubt that Terence Conran feels the need to cancel a trip to the theatre to go and help with a bit of washing up if the usual boy has overdone the E the night before, so there must come a point where you can avoid the responsibility again. I just hadn't reached that point yet.

Taking evenings off became too much of a hassle, so I lived my life the other way round to most people. Daytimes were my time for R'n'R, Friday afternoons were miserable as I contemplated a weekend of work, stress and hot grease, while Monday lunchtimes and evenings were my times for getting pissed and whooping it up, increasingly on my own.

Naomi and I had entered that stage of a relationship known as 'drifting apart'. We were still good friends and saw each other from time to time but it meant less. Occasionally she would join me at Beau's stable but, as she had a distrust of large rambunctious animals (including horses), these visits soon tailed off. Then, a month or two later she told me that she had started going out with another man. He was an electrician, kindly and with grown-up children of his own, who seemed happy to spend his evenings and weekends rewiring her house. There was talk, even, of his moving in.

The news really shouldn't have bothered me quite as much as it did.

It was not long after this discovery that I found myself chatting to a customer who'd nipped in to use the toilet and emerged extra-friendly one night. He pressed a couple of small pills into my hand, and thus began My Drugs Hell. As drugs hells go it didn't amount to much – I wasn't about to turn into Ozzy Osbourne. In fact, it amounted to little more than a succession of rather detached Mondays (still my only night off) wandering into dance clubs, buying God knows what from some shady character, jigging around a bit and maybe ending the evening with a one-night stand. Amazingly simple if you approach these things just a touch more callously. For a few weeks I was joined by another thirty-something friend who was going through a divorce, until we both realised the desperate innappropriateness of it all, and stopped. Thus ended My Drugs Hell.

I had hoped that I had managed to get through this rather embarrassing and scarily precocious midlife crisis without anyone noticing, but apparently not. Although nobody actually said anything, there was a suspicious tendency from friends and family to turn up on a Monday afternoon or suggest chores that would fill in those awkward free hours. Perfectly self-sufficient friends would suddenly need a lift somewhere or I'd be asked to 'nip up to Ikea' because it was hell to visit on the weekend.

The trouble was that there were so few things to do in Sussex on a Monday that even the most creative, well-intentioned planners-of-other-people's-spare-time would sooner or later run out of ideas. Not my sister, Louise, though. She had a trump card to play – a five-day-old Alsatian-cross puppy. Louise has the most touching faith in the power of animals to solve all human ills, and though she wasn't quite sure what the ill was at the time she was certain a puppy would get me squarely back on the tracks. She didn't say this, of course. In fact, all she said was, 'Chris, could you just look after this puppy for me while I go on holiday? It'll be no problem I'm sure,' and handed me the puppy, along with a bag of necessary supplies – powdered puppy food, a syringe, a bottle with a teat and some rolls of kitchen paper. Then, before I could even utter the words 'Oh, go on then' (I've always been a soft touch with puppies), my sister was striding back to her car.

The puppy, it transpired, had been chucked out of the 'nest' by its mother and, though my sister had tried covertly to reintroduce it, the mother was having none of it, and gently carried it out to the garden each time to die. Looking after it was felt to be beyond the remit of her holiday house/dogsitter, so I was to be its mother instead, and expected to feed it every two hours. I stared down at the little, squeaky, overactive slug-like creature she had entrusted me with and felt a twinge of pride at this sacred duty, and a curiosity to see how I got on in my brand new role – that of Alsatian-cross bitch.

As she revved the engine and started moving away, Louise explained what I would have to do. It seems that, to stimulate the puppy to feed, one must first stimulate it to do something at the other end (perhaps, I don't know, to create some kind of siphon effect). Every two hours, day and night, while warming a fresh batch of milk, I was to dip kitchen paper in tepid water and, holding the struggling little bundle of muscle securely in one hand, gently dab its bottom as though the kitchen paper were an Alsatian mother's tongue. Nice. Then I would wait for the desired effect, clear that up, pour some milk into the bottle, carefully checking the temperature, affix the teat, let the puppy do its stuff, and put it back in its bed somewhere warm, like the airing cupboard, or on top of the oven.

It would have been useless trying to explain that this whole process simply wasn't consistent with the hygiene requirements of a modern catering establishment and, anyway, Louise was halfway down the road by the time I thought of it, heading for a holiday cottage in France. So it was just the two of us. He was jet black, sleek and rather plump for a poor, abandoned foundling. I named him Biggie, after Biggie Smalls, the morbidly obese rapper. His eyes weren't open yet, and occasionally he would raise his head, whimper a bit and sniff the world, looking for mummy. Then he'd go back to sleep.

Looking after the little chap at home wasn't going to be a problem. Well, not a problem apart from the whole getting-up-every-two-hours thing, but at work was another matter. This being April, it was much too cold to put him out in the shed or in my car, so he'd have to come along to the Diner with me.

Animals and restaurants is a vexed issue. I once worked in a pub kitchen where the owner's two cats slunk about the place, always under my feet, meowing, scratching, licking and occasionally jumping onto the work surfaces looking for offcuts from the smoked salmon sandwiches. That sort of thing is frowned on these days. Indeed, modern attitudes have swung too far the other way, with dogs being barred even from sitting quietly under a table in a country pub, lest they somehow, as if by magic, slobber all over the food and poison us. Unless they're guide dogs, of course, which are okay.

Miss Green eschewed the use of guide dogs herself (I never discovered why) but a friend of hers would bring in her guide dog almost every day of a two-week visit, and the dog would make a beeline for any stray chips nestling under tables, dragging its poor owner across the floor (I thought that sort of thing was trained out of them). Personally, I can't see a dog without feeling the need to sit down with it and stroke it, although whenever this happened in the Diner I would have to make a great show of washing my hands afterwards and changing my apron so that none of the other customers would think we were unhygienic.

Biggie wasn't going to be a problem, though, so long as no one found out about him. I made a little bed from an empty tomato box, with a hot water bottle under a nice soft jumper, and put it under the counter. I should have remembered to warn Lucy he was there, if only to avoid her shrieking hysterically when she came across a large black rat lookalike, sleeping in a box under the counter.

The staff took to him, but only briefly. They cooed at him once, but thereafter maintained an attitude of mild disgust, and completely refused to help out at feeding time, when I would slip past the customers with Biggie concealed in my apron and avail myself of the baby-changing facility in the toilet. I soon learnt to spot when he was about to wake up, so I could pre-empt the appalling scream that the animal would launch into within seconds of awaking hungry and motherless. If I missed his cues I could be taking a customer's order when a noise like a Formula One car in distress would erupt from behind the bar. It's not an easy noise to explain away so, just in case, I turned the volume of the music up, while being careful to choose pup-friendly artists, since Biggie was sleeping next to the stereo. Music-wise, Biggie's namesake was much too loud and brash, as were most of the West Coast rappers, so we had to settle for more soulful artists, like David Gray or Dido.

My biggest fear was that an Environmental Health Officer might walk in unannounced. Their job is to ensure that the food we eat is prepared safely and in a manner not likely to poison us, which they do by periodic inspections of catering premises. But because there are so few inspectors they rarely visit more than once a year, and the rarity of these unexpected visits makes them all the more scary. To pre-empt this, whenever I felt a visit might be due I would ring up with some kind of banal query in the hope that they would tell me when they were coming and offer to discuss the issue then.

This tactic generally worked and, once inspectors feel you're on their side and take them seriously, they'll usually leave you alone for another year. Traditionally, EHOs had been in two minds as to whether to clean up catering by kind understanding and education or by wielding the big stick. But, due to a combination of lack of local government finance and the explosion in food outlets, they came to realise they'd never be able to keep up, so they began promoting the idea that keeping food clean is a team effort, sending out chatty newsletters with 'Germ of the Month!' (I kid you not) and 'Meet the Team!' features.

Which is not to say that EHOs have gone soft. They're a very professional bunch, mainly women – firm, efficient, and well aware of their brief so as not to give bad-tempered chefs any grounds for complaint on technical matters. And why should caterers get shirty, when the interest of the customer, caterer and EHO are the same? I often wondered, standing nervously behind as they burrowed about in my fridges, at their own personal practices and psychology. Were their kitchens scrupulously clean? If, say, the vicar came round for tea, and they realised their only pint of milk was possibly, arguably, on the turn, would they put it in the tea anyway? Also, were they clean and fastidious in everything they did, or in some matters a bit wild and grubby? I felt tempted to ask, but in Environmental Health matters, it's always advisable to keep conversation short, to the point and get them out the door as quickly as possible.

Anyway, the EHO was probably just as perplexed by the psychological make-up of the weirdo pacing nervously behind her, offering profuse and convoluted explanations for things that weren't wrong anyway.

As I had hoped, the nice lady at the council health department told me she could come down tomorrow to discuss my interesting query about new kitchen floor coverings, so I had plenty of time to prepare everything and get Biggie out the way, because, for all his lovable nature, I was pretty sure that the presence of a puppy under the counter would earn me the big stick.

The meeting went well. Biggie was safely out in the car, while Miss Marshall – a neat, youngish woman wearing thick spectacles and a lab coat – discussed flooring materials, side seams and drainage with me. Then, as I expected, she suggested getting the annual inspection out of the way. There was a sticky moment when she found Biggie's hot water bottle by the kettle, but I got away with it by explaining that I sometimes slept in the restaurant if I was too drunk to go home – I mean, too tired. (The problem with inspections is that you get so nervous you start coming up with ridiculous explanations for anything remotely odd, just in case the real reason is illegal. Though I suppose in this instance the real reason was illegal.)

The inspection concluded, Miss Marshall was taking off her white coat and folding it neatly as we left the kitchen, when she leant against a small shelf, eighteen inches by twelve, that was used to hold a box of raw chips next to the fryer. It wobbled. Not much, but there was definitely a wobble. 'That's a health and safety issue,' she commented. 'You'd better get it sorted out before someone gets injured.' I should have let it lie. The Golden Rule when dealing with EHOs is that you agree with absolutely

161

everything they say, at all times. What you don't ever do, under any circumstances, is laugh.

Miss Marshall glared at me through her glasses.

'Health and safety issues are no laughing matter, Mr Nye. You should know that.'

'But surely this is more of a small wobbly shelf issue?' I protested. 'How's it going to hurt anyone?'

Miss Marshall suddenly looked consumed with rage, though she managed to keep it in check as she icily enunciated the words: 'I will be back to check on your progress with the DANGEROUS shelf next week, Mr Nye.' And off she went. Bugger.

It wasn't just a wobbly shelf issue. Kitchen design is all about where to put things, and chefs can never have enough shelves. This may have been only a small shelf, but it was built to my own design by Ken, sized and positioned for maximum ergonomic efficiency when putting chips in the fryer, which I had to do about 300 times a day. It was collapsible for ease of cleaning the fryer, and of a robust melamine construction with stout easy-clean hinges. Perfect, in a word. But even I had to agree that it wobbled. In fact, periodically I would unscrew it from the wall, put in a larger rawlplug and rescrew it, where it would sit proudly wobble-free for at least a couple of weeks until it started wobbling again.

Now I would have to get a man in to fix the shelf – a proper man that is, with a toolbox – and organise an escape route for Biggie when Mrs Marshall returned unexpectedly. Meanwhile, the pressure of 2, 4 and 6am feeds was taking its toll, leaving me wandering round like a zombie.

On the bright side, Biggie put on some weight and his eyes started to open a little. Laura and Sally almost began to like him, as I caught them surreptitiously giving him a little stroke or tickle when they thought I wasn't watching. Then he became ill. Never the most expressive of pets, he was downcast and list-

162

less; uninterested in his surroundings or the morsels of rice pudding I tried to tempt him with. At first I put it down to too much David Gray and Lighthouse Family, but the vet felt it was probably some sort of bug.

This was a problem. Puppies per se were bad enough, especially with a prowling Miss Marshall, but a puppy with a tummy bug was an invitation to disaster. Suppose Uckfield lost thousands to a mystery plague, eventually traced to a small diner and the owner's misguided loyalty to an Alsatian-cross pup?

It was Silvio who came up with a solution: some kind of cloche to protect Biggie from the harmful effects of smoke and noise, while protecting us from the bacteria spewing out of Biggie. I nipped down to the garden centre and bought a puppy-sized plant propagator, lined it with my softest jumper and threw in a few of Biggie's toys (though he no longer seemed well enough to be interested in either his pink ball or bendy yellow bone). So Biggie slept under the counter in his very own incubator, looking like a horribly premature baby or a very ripe cheeseboard, while I gazed in lovingly every ninety seconds or so.

As the restaurant started filling up on his first incubator evening, Biggie started moving around. Or at least his top half did, sitting up on his front paws and swaying like a seal, only with a frothing mouth. It was such an upsetting sight that soon I could stand it no longer and, abandoning the customers to Silvio's cooking, I grabbed the propagator and ran up the High Street to the vet's surgery. The sympathetic Australian vet said that mother animals have an instinct for these things and there was probably something very wrong with this puppy. She suggested the kindest thing to do was to put him down. I couldn't bear to let him die in a cold, miserable surgery, though, so I took him home with me. The rest of the evening I closed the Diner 'due to staff illness' for the very first time, and sat at home watching the television with Biggie.

The next morning he was looking a little better and, as if to cap the sense that a corner had been turned, I had a call from Liz to say that Miss Marshall had swept in that very morning and declared herself satisfied with the maintenance of the shelf. Over the next few days Biggie returned to normal health. Vets, eh?

My sister returned home the following week, wondering why I looked so haggard, and pleased to reunite Biggie with his brothers and sisters. He ended up living on a farm near Uckfield – and not in a 'Sit down kids, I've something to tell you. You know that little Fluffy who was a bit poorly? Well, he's gone to live on a farm' sort of way, either. He ended up guarding a farm, because, his social skills being severely impaired by his difficult start in life, Biggie became the doggie equivalent of Gary B, and reputedly one of the meanest guard dogs in Sussex.

Can't complain

BIGGIE'S ILLNESS COINCIDED WITH THAT YEAR'S OSCARS, in which *Shakespeare in Love* cleaned up. Meantime in Brighton, Famous Moes, a local pizza chain, won a PAPA, awarded by the Pizza and Pasta Association to the National Pizza Shop of the Year. I knew this because they had emblazoned 'National Pizza Shop of the Year' across every menu and shopfront. And who could blame them? It would have been nice if there was an equivalent award ceremony recognising supreme quality in the burger trade – a BAP, perhaps, presented by the Burger and Pie Association – but sadly it was not to be. There were the Cateys, of course, awarded by the *Caterer and Hotelkeeper* magazine, but they were a bit hifalutin and I couldn't imagine us pipping the Roux family and their ilk to a prize. But the PAPAs gave me an idea: why not launch an award ourselves and get some good, cheap publicity? Thus were conceived the Maximum Diner Favourite Customer of the Year Awards.

We had 1200 delivery addresses on file, so there were plenty of people to consider. But, as I looked through them with a view to compiling the requisite longlist, I realised to my dismay that almost 80 percent of them had only ordered once or twice. It's always nice to see Pareto's Law so beautifully illustrated in a practical context, but it didn't say much for our service. Apparently, nearly 1000 Uckfield households were philosophically comfortable with the concept of getting fast food delivered, and had even taken the psychologically huge next step of choosing what to order, picking up the phone, getting the money ready, waiting for it, and (hopefully) putting it on a plate and eating it. And had then chosen not to do so again.

For all I know, one in five might be well above the industry standard for repeat custom but it struck me as embarrassing, and seemed to cast aspersions on our food. Maybe that's why I didn't have a chain of shops yet. And then I thought about all those places I had loved on my first visit, and had resolved to go back to, then simply never got round to it. There was Bill's Cafe in Lewes, Gordon Ramsay's (I wasn't paying), the Madonna Inn in California, and a host of other things like *Les Miserables*, or the mountainous bit of Slovenia... in fact, when I analysed it, my fondness for a place seemed to have absolutely no statistical correlation with whether I ever went back there. If anything I tended to see the nicest places as so special that I wouldn't want to risk over-use.

166 So that was it! The Maximum Diner was so special that people were putting it in a kind of special box for special things only to be used on special occasions. That made me feel pretty special, too, and the Maximum Diner Favourite Customer of the Year Awards could be a means of paying some of that back, while also suggesting that, extra-special as we were, it was still okay to use us on a daily basis; we wouldn't mind. So we started sorting out the prize letters.

Everyone, we decided, would be a winner – well, almost everyone. The roll call read like this:

1st =

> *The lovely newlyweds in Barnet Way*
>
> *Dani and Dave (obviously)*
>
> *Ebony (unofficial most beautiful woman in Uckfield)*
>
> *Mr Young (kind, supportive, high-spending) and his really
> nice family (all of them) in West Park*
>
> *Fat Harry (let's keep him sweet)*
>
> *Robbo's girlfriend Marie (for having a baby and curtailing
> his violence for a while)*
>
> *Julian and his trust fund (for keeping his stoned mates in
> munchies every night)*
>
> *The lady in the High Street everyone thought had become
> an alcoholic and an embarrassment to her friends and
> neighbours, but was then diagnosed with a brain tumour,
> operated on and became normal again (hurrah!)*
>
> *The lady in the satin nightie at Streatfield Road*
>
> *The gay couple at Tower Ride with the exceptionally cool
> taste in shirts*
>
> *The customer who didn't kick up a fuss when a new
> delivery driver handed over some food and then vomited
> on his doorstep (car sick, apparently; the driver didn't
> stay long)*
>
> *The lady in the satin nightie at Streatfield Road*

167

and many more in the same vein. They all received, not a trophy,
but much better – a free tub of Häagen-Dazs with their next
order (over £10). Really, it was the thought that counted.

Inevitably these top awards were skewed towards Adam's list of
Sexy Customers and Big Tippers, though I'm not sure what
other criteria might have been taken into account. Everyone else
came second or third (equal), apart from those customers who

we hated – each of whom received a letter informing them that they'd come 1117th in the Maximum Diner Favourite Customer of the Year Awards and were therefore ineligible for a prize. This might seem petty-minded, vindictive even, and was certainly out of keeping with the spirit of the prize-giving, but it was a huge pleasure nonetheless. Being allowed to give free rein to your antipathies is one of the very few pure joys of owning your own business. And some customers clearly deserve to be told just how rubbish they are, foremost among them the ones who have the temerity to complain about their food.

The textbook method of dealing with a customer who is com-plaining (and you will be taught this at catering college) is to go to their table and crouch down so that your elbows are on the table and your own head is slightly lower than the customer's. Listen to the complaint without interrupting, while maintaining eye contact (except for occasionally looking downwards, as if deeply disappointed). Apologise. Ask how you can make it up to them. Rip up the bill and then remedy the situation so that you're never left in such a horrible position ever again.

But there are several problems with the textbook version. Firstly, the customers aren't usually out of a textbook them-selves; secondly, complaints tend to happen when things are going badly and you're stressed, sweaty, and rushing about like the proverbial part-blue fly; and thirdly, IT'S NOT YOUR FUCKING FAULT the waitress hasn't turned up! So the most common responses when dealing with complaints are: (a) blame yourself, perhaps dramatically bursting into tears; (b) blame the customer; or (c) blame a third party – suppliers, the waitress who's mixed her shifts up, the weather, Wealden District Council, Europe... anything really.

This defensiveness may come from the fact that catering is often seen as a menial job, yet people feel entirely free to launch criticisms at its workers. Perhaps there's a prejudice lingering from the industry's roots 'in service' to the gentry, or perhaps it's part of a latent racism because so many workers in the industry are foreign. Whatever the reason, the British seem to think it shows admirable assertiveness to complain in restaurants. It's true that the majority still prefer to leave muttering quietly under their breath, but there's a certain type of self-satisfied person for whom complaining appeals. Unsurprisingly, these are exactly the ones that the complainee is least likely to want to prostrate themselves before. As Groucho Marks might have put it, I wouldn't want to apologise to any customer who was so rude as to complain.

I suspect even more people might complain if they weren't just a tiny bit worried about what chefs will do to their food out of view in the kitchen. On this I can reassure them that I've never seen anyone do anything horrible to anyone's food – hardly ever. The stories, though, are rife of chefs sending steaks out which are certainly better done, but have also been used as something between a loofah and a J-cloth while waiting to be plated (you'll have to use your imagination). If half of what we hear is true, Michael Winner probably wouldn't still be alive.

It's not just the complainers, however, who upset the mild-mannered caterer. There are other culprits too. A customer that no caterer likes is the first one of the day. You've spent the early morning rushing to keep on schedule, trying to get organised for a busy day, or you've finally got ready and are enjoying a private moment with a bacon sandwich and the newspaper, when someone puts their head round the back door and says, 'Coo-ee! Are you open yet?' It's generally not until the third or fourth customer that I can bring myself to be pleasant, and then I try to overcompensate for my earlier surliness.

The last customer is rarely too popular, either; the one who comes in just when you've got everything cleaned up ready for a nice quick getaway. Customers who order the most boring item on the menu are beneath contempt, but are nowhere near as annoying as those who brightly say, 'Got any specials on today?', the implication being that what's on the menu just isn't special enough. And then, of course, there are the nutters, against whom, even when the insults are raining down, the caterer's main weapon is to keep a sense of humour. One perfectly normal-looking man dialled 999 on my phone and asked for the police because he claimed his burger didn't have enough lettuce in it. A policewoman turned up, calmly examined the burger and told the man that she thought the salad item was sufficient, but if he was still dissatisfied he could always take the offending object to the small claims court. Oblivious to her irony the man picked up his now-wilted shred of lettuce, brandished it like a gauntlet I had thrown down, and warned me that I had by no means seen the last of it. I'm quite looking forward to seeing that lettuce again, actually.

Some restaurateurs – or, more likely, their area managers – would react with horror to any idea that the customer isn't always right. Customers, especially the regulars, are supposed to be treated with the same respect that you'd pay visiting royalty. Although, to my mind, that makes it even more insulting for them to complain, a terrible breach of etiquette, tantamount to shoving silverware up their sleeve at a foreign state banquet. And, it has to be said, there comes a point in every caterer's career when there's no choice left but to tell a customer to fuck off. The industry has yet to set a standard for judging this; it's more a question of instinct, and there are many variables to be balanced – most notably, potential for violence and whether or not they've paid.

170

Normally, and for obvious reasons, the types who complain tend not to become regulars, although there are a few who slip through the net and this creates a bit of a dilemma. Regulars, as we've already ascertained, are the bedrock of a business so there's absolutely every reason to tolerate their little ways (with the exception, of course, of The Three Garys' and Robbo's little ways). But, yobbery apart, in my seven years of running the Diner there was only one regular I unequivocally detested. The customer's name was Jonathan, and he used to come in every Sunday afternoon.

In the early days, Jonathan was tolerable, aside from an unfortunate resemblance to Sebastian Coe. (He wore the petulant, sullen expression that Coe made famous on the podium for his 800m Bronze Medal at the 1980 Moscow Olympics – an obscure reference but, trust me, that was the look.) No, initially the problem was his bossy, blonde Aryan wife, a determined lady (nothing wrong with that) who once nearly caused a fight by telling another customer not to put money in the jukebox while she was eating. This prompted two other tables of people to hum exaggeratedly loudly, between stifled giggles, while I ducked down behind the counter trying to hide, so as not to be called on to intervene. Jonathan stopped coming in after that, until one evening several months later, when he arrived with another woman, a slightly mousy, younger version of himself with a voice so quiet we had to ask her to repeat everything nine times before eventually turning to Jonathan for a dubbed version.　171

Jonathan, by contrast, was a man transformed. It was no more Mr Nice Guy. Free at last, he was determined to reorganise the world to his own satisfaction. At first it was flattering. He seemed to really love the Diner and, as with all our regular customers, I felt a sense of gratitude that he had repeatedly chosen my place to eat. But soon the familiar old Diner was no longer enough for him; he began to want to make little changes. This can happen with even quite nice regulars: they get bored with the humble role of consumer and start wanting to play a more active part. Like a new girlfriend who starts chucking out your old cardies and buying you roll-neck sweaters, they start mixing dishes, having starters as main courses and main courses as starters, ordering things 'on the side'; replacing that with this and this with that. But Jonathan took it to new heights. For instance, one day he asked me if I could rustle him up some fresh buttered peas. Not an unreasonable request, you might suppose, but I scanned the menu and... no... no buttered peas seemed to be listed. So where, at 5.30pm on a Sunday evening did he suppose I was going to get some peas from? From the magic pea bush?

It became clear that Jonathan was outstaying his welcome. He had taken to coming in twice a day, each time rearranging the Diner to his own personal satisfaction and to hell with anyone else. The music had to go down, the heating had to go up. If he couldn't have his usual table he would tut loudly and stare at the people who were sitting at it. He insisted on having his order taken by me instead of the waitress. Rather than taking a paper off the rack like everyone else did, he would call a member of staff over, tell that staff member to go over to the newspaper rack and advise him of what was available; he would then choose, and staff member would bring the chosen newspaper over to him. It was funny for a while, but eventually he started to annoy the other customers.

172   Credit where credit's due, though – for it was Gary A who finally solved that particular problem for me.

Late one snowy winter's night Jonathan had, as usual, left his four-by-four outside the shop on hazard lights instead of parking it in the layby fifteen feet away. As he and the girlfriend ate their meal, Gary and co came in, ordered their food and went out for a snowball fight, as you do. Jonathan's girlfriend seized her chance to release a bit of tension and swept into action, yelling at them in a surprisingly loud voice not to go near her off-roader with any snow. There followed a stunned pause, as five yobs took this in, then a great cheer and the relentless crump of snowball on car. Jonathan leapt up, reached over the counter for my phone and demanded I dialled 999.

Well, the story of Matilda sprang to mind: if people kept calling the police to help with lettuce deficiency and snowball emergencies, they wouldn't be in such a hurry when Guppy decided to deep-fry my head. So I told him not to be so silly and pointed out that he was illegally parked anyway.

Stomping out, for the last time, Jonathan ranted at Gary, 'I hope your balls fall off,' to which Gary replied, 'Yeah, in your girlfriend's mouth.' Not exactly a Wildean exchange perhaps, but one that I enjoyed nonetheless. We never saw Jonathan again, and I never got any more trouble from that particular crowd of hooligans.

Meanwhile, as if to show that we could manage perfectly happily without the likes of Jonathan and his girlfriend, trade was going from good to great. As well as the hundreds of deliveries we were doing each week, the restaurant was getting filled up at least twice a day. I never felt satisfied with a shift unless I'd experienced the pleasant sensation of being unable to cope.

It was time to expand our operation. I started looking for other towns to open another diner in, Lewes being the most obvious as it was halfway between Brighton and Uckfield and its demographics were perfect. The problem was that the Maximum Diner I already had only ran so smoothly because I was working in it all the time and because I had such uniquely wonderful employees. My restaurant had all those little foibles and quirks that you get in an owner-managed business: a temperamental

173

boiler that only *I* could get hot water out of, a fryer that tripped out and had to be precariously rewired in situ every other week, cash kept in a biscuit tin. Chain businesses, even two-outlet chains, rely on a simplicity of operation such that it's almost impossible to do the job wrong. So if I opened another diner in the same style I would need to invest to simplify and standard-ise everything in both places so that customers would get exact-ly the same service and food. On top of which, my costs would escalate. Although I was taking £4000 a week now, mysteriously little ended up as bottom-line profit, whereas I needed to be get-ting enough in profit to pay a manager, pay my salary while I opened a new outlet, and offer a good return to any prospective 'business angel'.

Alternatively, I could enjoy the success of the Diner and relax, stop endlessly striving for success and wealth, and appreciate the good things in life. It was tempting. I shelved the expansion of the Maximum franchise for a year.

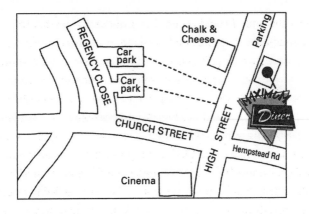

Uckfield, c'est moi!

WHILE A SMALL PAT ON THE BACK definitely seemed in order, my decision to put the expansion plans on hold kept me awake at nights. I couldn't help but feel I'd stopped slightly short of my ambitions. The Diner was doing well but was I really content to drift along in our little comfort zone, making enough money to pay the immediate bills but never quite enough to go national, nor laying much aside for a rainy day? Was I really happy to stop at one outlet? Suppose Mr Budgen had just opened one small shop and then put his feet up? It was a sobering thought.

Day to day, though, the business could hardly have been better. Liz was doing a brilliant job of boosting our daytime trade and had even persuaded me to take on yet another customer to help with the extra work. She was a young Senegalese woman called Beatrice who used to come in with her two young children and, unlike anyone else we'd employed, had actually trained and worked as a professional cook. At last our proud boast that 'Our staff are polite and welcoming and one of them once did a catering course' was true. Liz, Laura, Sally and I would watch in awe as Beatrice swung into action at the start of her shift, rearranging the kitchen, preparing ingredients with deft chops and scrapes (using a knife she brought in herself) and then conjuring cooked burgers as if from thin air.

Adam, meanwhile, had shelved his own dreams to be a surfer-cum-sports psychologist and was seriously considering chiropody. Not an obvious career shift, perhaps, but it had a certain logic. It all began when he saw the film *Jerry Maguire* and decided to be a sport's agent instead. After discussing this with his very patient career guidance counsellor, he decided that maybe he should settle for being a sports physiotherapist instead. Then he spoke to the colleges offering courses in physiotherapy, who considered his qualifications and suggested he try something else. 'What about podiatry?' they suggested.

'Podiatry?' he asked.

'Yes, podiatry. It's like physiotherapy, but for feet' They replied.

'Feet?!' He shrieked. 'I'm not touching people's feet!'

Over the next few days we all chuckled along with Adam at the prospect of him becoming a specialist foot therapist, until Liz pointed out that he might rather like spending his working days kneeling in front of sporty women in tennis skirts, massaging their feet. You could almost see a lightbulb switching on over Adam's head as he considered the possibility, and the next day he called the colleges again, begging to be let on the course.

Whether he blew it at the interview by going on and on too enthusiastically about tennis, I don't know, but Adam was rejected by all the podiatry schools. However, having broken down the psychological barrier of treating feet he didn't seem able to let it go, and started asking us all whether we didn't think that chiropody would be just as good really; indeed, if anything a bit less

176

boringly technical and more excitingly 'hands on'? I'm not above putting staff off career changes just to keep them working for me, but I felt on safe grounds steering Adam away from this one. Besides I was going to need him to help with an idea that was just beginning to form in my mind.

It had started with Adam anyway. He had attended the grand opening of Uckfield's new skateboard ramp, at which the local MP, Jeffrey Johnson-Smith (very old-school Tory, think Iain Duncan-Smith crossed with Leslie Phillips) had made a speech, cut a ribbon, and then stood huddling for warmth with some local councillors in the cold of a February day while a couple of kids in baggy trousers went up and down and up and down the ramp. 'It needed something to make it all more of an occasion,' said Adam, afterwards. 'Hey, you should have been selling burgers down there!'

I wasn't convinced that the presence of a burger van would have added much to the grandness or gaiety of the occasion, but even so it was worth considering. After all, what did a band do when it wanted to promote itself? It went on the road. What did a political leader do during an election? Got himself a battlebus. Here was our chance to get the name 'Maximum Diner' out amongst the people, and give Burger Off a right good kicking into the bargain. Every car boot sale, we would be there. Every school fête, every village bonfire, every local football derby, the Mobile Maximum Diner would be there. 'On the beach?' asked Adam. 'Yes Adam, why not?' We could go anywhere. I began getting seriously enthused.

But why limit ourselves to local events? And what about taking hash out to the people, as well? I was picturing a chef in a van, behind a great expanse of hot metal, expertly stir-frying potato

177

hash in front of the slavering crowds. The chef would have a big pile of onions and peppers and potato sizzling away and, as the next hungry patron reached the front of the queue and ordered, say, chicken barbecue hash, the chef would separate a portion of the mix out from the pile, bung some chicken on, stir it in with a couple of nimble flicks of the spatula, splatter on the barbecue sauce, chuck it in a box, plastic fork and on to the next customer. Bish bosh – £3.95. Over and over again. No washing up; no hassle. Suppose we had a van at the Glastonbury Festival saying in big wobbly, psychedelic letters, 'Hashman!' or 'Hash, man'? We'd be mobbed.

My whole body quivered in anticipation of this bold new expansion scheme, and I launched into two days of frantic activity. Certain parts of the operation would have to be delegated. Adam, while occasionally allowing his mind to wander a bit off the job, had a spark of common sense beneath it all, and whoever was stuck in the van (I mean, responsible for this arm of the business) would have to be utterly trustworthy. They wouldn't need to be a great chef, just efficient, hard-working, and if they were a bit cool and could banter a bit with the customers then so much the better. Now, it is said that if you want to motivate your staff, you don't give them a raise, you give them a title. So I sat down with Adam, and told him I'd like him to consider taking the post of Head of Distribution (UK). He was up for it, so together we set about finding a van.

178   When it comes to catering vans, you can go for self-propelled, as it were, or trailers. As we stood on various windy garage forecourts looking at vans, I had to drag Adam away from top-of-the-range models with bunks, toilets and four-wheel-drive (for getting to those tricky point-to-points and muddier festivals) that cost rather more than a house, and back to the more modest trailers with a griddle and somewhere to stand while cooking on it. I didn't have the money yet even for one of these, but felt

that the banks would be sure to lend on the basis of such a terrific, foolproof idea.

It would need a separate business plan, so Adam and I went down to 'gather intelligence' from the sharp-looking bloke with a burger van who parked outside the local DIY superstore in Uckfield's industrial estate on weekdays. Apparently he made a reasonable living from servicing visiting builders and local workers. And so it was that, for the second time in my life, I received information from a man in a van that would transform my career. I had casually asked him how business was going.

'Not bad, really,' he sighed, 'but I'm a bit worried about what I'm going to do when McDonald's opens.'

'Eh? What? McDonald's?' I stuttered.

'Yeah,' he said, 'Opening next to Tesco's. It's all just going through now.'

Oh shit, I thought.

I'd seen reports in the press about the aggressive expansion plans of the world's greatest fast food merchant, but the trade papers are always full of this or that chief executive fat cat justifying a multi-million pay hike with the promise of opening hundreds of new stores, so I wasn't too bothered. Anyway, why would they come to Uckfield? This was burger van territory; much too insignificant for their style of operation.

But the simple answer was that McDonald's have to expand. They realised long ago what I had only just discovered that, to survive long term, any business must stay dynamic, innovating, expanding and getting into new markets all the time. Uckfield was their new front line.

As news of the proposed opening spread, customers I bumped into in aisle three at Tesco's would shake their heads wistfully, avoid eye contact and mutter, 'Those utter bastards,' then extend a hand and give my shoulder a sympathetic, encouraging squeeze before walking quietly away.

But how long had I got before they opened? The man to ask was Uckfield's property-dealing honcho, Mr Lawson, of Lawson Commercial. If you want to buy or sell any commercial property in Uckfield, you'll need to speak to Chris Lawson; his name hangs above almost every empty or struggling shop in Uckfield and its surrounding area. He's a friendly, helpful, prosperous-looking chap, who, being bald on top and with big sideburns, looks quite Dickensian. I could imagine previous generations of Victorian Lawsons running the town's mill or sitting on the workhouse charitable committee.

I went round to Mr Lawson's office on the pretext of discussing the Diner and, while fending off his three intrusively friendly dogs, explained that I was thinking of selling and, incidentally, what was happening about McDonald's?

What I could glean – and this was my interpretation, not his – was that negotiations had been going on for two years while wily McDonald's pressured brave, plucky Wealden Council into granting planning permission. Perhaps I'd been wrong about Wealden Planning, who were not after all meddling, jumped-up busybodies but tireless heroes, a Thin Green Line against the forces of burger imperialism. However, a deal had finally been reached and the building would soon start.

Within two days everything was announced in the *Uckfield Sussex Express*. McDonald's was going to build a new Drive-thru on Uckfield's busiest, most gridlocked roundabout between Tesco's and the industrial estate, on the flat bit of town by the river. If this was what the council had been negotiating over for two years I dread to imagine what the original McDonald's plan was, because (and I accept I'm biased here) it struck me as a disaster for the town.

180

It seemed, however, that I held the minority view. A reporter from the *Independent on Sunday* rang for some comments, pointing out that there seemed to be a bit of a contrast between Hampstead, whose residents had fiercely opposed the opening of a new McDonald's in their High Street, and Uckfield, where she understood the council was planning to welcome their new restaurant with a parade? Did I have a view?

Despite years of protests, McDonald's were finally allowed to open a store in rich, leafy Hampstead under the proviso that it was nice and subtle and carefully designed to be in keeping with the rest of the High Street. Perhaps they offered to serve organic *McGoatscheeseburgers* and hand-carve the golden arches in reclaimed walnut wood that had been artistically distressed. In Uckfield permission had been granted to throw up a plastic drive-thru that would dominate the centre of the town and bring traffic to a standstill. So much for Wealden Planners.

The tone of the journalist's questioning suggested that she thought we were a bunch of unsophisticated yokels – an image somewhat reinforced by the Mayor, who was quoted as saying what an honour it was to welcome 'the first drive-thru in the Weald', that this was fantastic news for Uckfield because it would really put the town 'on the map'. What map would that be then, I wanted to know? Anyway, I couldn't help but wonder why, if he loved burgers so much, the Mayor had never made it into my place. But I wasn't bitter, oh no. I had to play it cool, appearing unruffled by the competition and pointing out that I was all for more accessible, affordable places for families to enjoy a tasty meal out without being convinced that McDonald's was the best solution for Uckfield.

Bad though it was for me, at least I was at the other end of town. It was worse for poor Hagrid at Burger Off, which was a mere twenty-five yards from the site, where construction had started with a large McDonald's customer car park being laid out and landscaped. However, he too was trying to sound upbeat, giving customers his own version of 'We will fight them on the beaches.' I was hoping he'd make a more powerful statement, maybe in the style of Jose Bove, the French militant farmer who flattened a half-built McDonald's with a JCB, or at least that he'd go for a long, slow conscience-pricking decline culminating in a 'dirty protest' while perched on the top of one of the golden arches themselves. But the guy clearly had no sense of the dramatic and he was pre-empted in any case by his landlord selling the shop from under him for use as a bus shelter. Conspiracy? I couldn't possibly say that, but we were denied the happy sight of Man Mountain taking on the skinny girl who arrived to become the manager of McDonald's, getting her face in the paper as the McDonald's public relations department swung into action.

At least Burger Off's demise had been quick and painless. I foresaw a long, lingering death for the Maximum Diner, as customers gradually drifted away, seduced by McDonald's easy parking, toys for the kids, and close proximity to Tesco's. We would become like the nearby butchers at the top of the High Street: friendly staff offering high-quality produce that people promised to support, but in reality only visited at Christmas, muttering that the little shop was really much too expensive but they felt they should support it. Customers tried to be supportive, gamely telling me that they personally hated McDonald's and certainly wouldn't be going there. Then they'd order a Big Mac and fries. 'Big Max,' I'd correct them, 'with chips?' and they'd say yeah, that's what they'd meant to say.

182

Pointless though it seemed, I felt I had to fight back, to begin the spark of protest. If the town council was going to capitulate, fine. I, however, was made of sterner stuff: like General DeGaulle, I was nailing my colours to the mast and saying, 'Uckfield, c'est moi!' And I was not altogether alone in my resistance. A letter in that week's *Sussex Express* expressed my point of view perfectly. A certain Harriet Wheeler pointed out that 'drive-thrus' were an American idea that developed naturally and perfectly sensibly in a vast country with oodles of space where people have to drive around in order to get anywhere. But Uckfield is a small compact town with a High Street, in an overcrowded corner of an overcrowded island. As more people are encouraged to use cars to visit stores in trading estates, then the High Street will become increasingly redundant. Perhaps, she suggested, that was why Uckfield now has *six* charity shops in its once thriving shopping centre. Harriet also mentioned the town's home-grown talent, including the Maximum Diner, which was very kind of her.

The next week another letter appeared in the *Express*, this time a congratulation to the Mayor for bringing in McDonald's. A Mr Roger Kirkwood had been giddy with excitement to read about the McDonald's development and shared both the Mayor and Chris Lawson's hope that this would once and for all put Uckfield 'on the map'. Because Uckfield wasn't really on the map at all right now, but with our very own McDonald's that problem would be rectified. Quite obviously it was the lack of wafer-thin slices of grated cow, microwaved to perfection, that had been holding this town back for so long...

Okay, I confess. I was both Roger Kirkwood and Harriet Wheeler (I nicked her name from The Sundays, whose CD I was listening to while composing my letters), and I was also Dinsdale Ragg, Rolf Ruff and Dr Veronica Trimbush, who wrote mourning the loss of Burger Off, and asked how much more of our home-grown talent would disappear before 'this madness ends'. But my letter-writing campaign failed to spark wider revolt. It seemed that I was the sole opposition to McDonald's: a one-man pressure group, exerting absolutely no pressure whatsoever.

183

Who was I kidding? Uckfield couldn't wait for McDonald's. The town was gagging for it.

The immediate fallout from McDonald's imminent arrival was that I had to shelve the van idea. There was an equally strong argument in favour of speeding up diversification, since the eat-in burger trade was obviously going to get sticky for the foreseeable future, but my designated business banker didn't see it that way. 'Consolidation, old boy,' he said, showing me the door. 'That's what we need now.'

So with no money to fund the project, I organised a meeting with Adam that was likely to be embarrassing. I was about to tell him that his 'distribution' duties would once again be limited to delivering burgers, but he looked even more nervous than me and, apologising profusely, said he had decided to begin training as a fitness instructor. I was not only enormously relieved, but genuinely delighted that he had found a career that suited him so well – 'Toning-up sweaty women in Lycra,' as he explained it.

Over the next couple of months I was treated to regular updates on the progress of building work, as people popped their head in the door and said, 'They've just put the roof on,' or 'The golden arches are up, and they revolve!', and I would try to adopt a posture of aloof dismissal, tutting irritably. I felt like a prisoner on death row watching through the bars of my cell as the scaffold they're going to hang me from is being built.

Meanwhile, I tried to cheer myself and the staff up by pointing to the takings graph, which was reaching unprecedented heights, the red line shooting through the top of the paper and halfway up the wall it was Blu-Tacked to. It was ironic that this should be one of the side-effects of McDonald's being built. People driving past obviously thought, 'Hmm, I'd love a Happy Meal right now!

184

But they're not open yet, so I suppose I'll just have to settle for a Surly Burger from the Maximum Diner,' and so they did. I knew this was happening because of the number of toddlers being dragged in wailing, 'WANNA GO TO MCDONALD'S WANNA GO TO MCDONALD'S WANNA GO TO MCDONALD'S,' with their parents yelling back, 'WE CAN GO THERE NEXT WEEK BUT WE HAVE TO COME HERE THIS WEEK, poppet.' A little humbling, that.

So, as sales records were smashed on a daily basis, and customers crowded in, I mentally ticked them off into Likely to go to McDonald's next week or Unlikely to go to McDonald's next week camps. On balance the likelies had it, but one group I hoped I could put on my side was a wedding party who arrived late one Saturday night asking if we could fit them in, as their reception was finished but they didn't want to go home yet. The bride and groom settled into a booth, her veil rubbing against a blackboard and turning multicoloured while the guests filled every other available seat. I popped out to get champagne and then did my party piece, slicing the tops of the bottles clean off with one stroke of a large carving knife, like French Hussars used to do with their sabres. I'd like to see them do that at McDonald's.

I began to wonder whether this wasn't going to be our salvation. Not post-wedding receptions per se, but abandoning the 'fast food with a cheeky grin' approach and aiming more for the bistro market. So I was a little bit happier as we finally saw the bride and groom off in the early hours, tottering down the High 185 Street holding each other up. I thought, 'Now that, is going to be a great marriage,' and decided to take their happiness as a good omen.

The good feeling didn't last. At the end of the week I had to endure the opening of McDonald's.

It has to be said that, compared to the opening of the first Beijing McDonald's, where thousands waited patiently for hours, or their Kuwait drive-thru, where the queue extended seven miles, Uckfield's Big Mac Day was a total washout. By the town's standards, though, it was a day to remember. It was the Friday of the August Bank Holiday, the sun was shining, bunting was blowing in a warm breeze, the kids were off school, and motorists stuck in traffic on the bypass wound their windows down to hear the odd snatch of feedback from the PA as the Mayor cleared his throat and welcomed McDonald's to town.

There followed a corporate donation to the Fourth Uckfield Scout Group, then a competition-winning cub cut the ceremonial ribbon and then led the whole pack in to receive a free meal. Is that what Lord Baden-Powell really had in mind, I wondered, when he formed the organisation? I was head sixer in my cub troop, the First Henfield, but I don't remember us standing on parade for just anyone. When did the Cubs or Brownies become a gun for hire? I wanted to call Brown Bloody Owl and give her a piece of my mind. Then again, I had to avoid appearing 'sad'.

Not that anyone would have noticed, for the scout ceremony was the cue for the town to take leave of its collective senses. McDonald's had put up signs along the bypass directing all the traffic that they expected to come from miles around, and their predictions were spot on as whole families arrived in people carriers and vans for a day out. A TV crew and all the local papers turned up to interview customers. Beatrice's two young children were so excited that she had to order a taxi to take them round the drive-thru facility.

I sat at the other end of the High Street in my empty shop and read the paper. The day before had been our busiest Thursday ever, and this was our quietest Friday ever. For a nanosecond I even considered staying open until midnight and serving alcohol to yobs again, as if I hadn't got enough problems.

I needed to pull something out of the hat, but what precisely? There was no point in advertising against McDonald's – they were getting so much press that our little 'Hey look at us! We're still here!' adverts would have been like waving a flag in space. No, my one previous hope was that McDonald's wouldn't sell quite enough for their style of continuous cooking, whereby your burger is put on the grill before you arrive on the basis that you (or someone) is sure to be arriving in time to eat it. Without a certain throughput of customers the system becomes either too wasteful or the food has to be cooked to order, which is precisely what customers don't want. And, if that were to happen, then McDonald's might pull out.

Some hope! Before the month was out spies told me that it was taking as much per hour as any other branch in the country, while our turnover was stuck at about half its pre-McDonald's level. It was clear that the Maximum Diner's successes were all in the past.

Underneath the (Golden) Arches

'THERE'S A TIME TO LEAN, and there's a time to... what, Laura?' 'Clean, Chris.' 'That's right, Laura. There's a time to lean, and there's a time to clean.'

That's how it was in the first few weeks after McDonald's opened. I rushed round motivating the staff like some over-enthusiastic second lieutenant trying to get the troops to go over the top. But that was then, and five months on it was all rather different.

'Chriiiiiis? 'Chriiii-iiis? Have you got anything else you want me to clean?' Laura's voice reached me as I lay dozing at the back of the restaurant, stretched out on a banquette, my head under a table. I sat up whoozily and tried to concentrate.

'You could clean the chewing gum from the bottom of this table.'

Laura grimaced. There was an agreement that I did any really unpleasant jobs, like unblocking toilets, clearing up sick and scraping chewing gum from where forgetful youths had left it under tables. This policy dated from a rash comment that I wouldn't expect my staff to do anything I wouldn't do myself, which somehow got translated into 'Chris does all the horrible jobs.' She sat beside me now, lit a cigarette, and offered me one. I had restarted smoking as a way of passing the time.

The Diner was spotless anyway. The equipment, the walls, ceiling, signs, light fittings, light bulbs, chair legs, bottoms of jars, tops of pictures, leaves of pot plants, telephones, CD covers, everything – it had all been cleaned and buffed and rebuffed and polished into a new dimension of cleanliness. There was nothing else to do, and the gungho spirit of before had been replaced with a kind of terminal laziness.

I had tried rereading Sun Tsu, and made no more headway with it than the first time. I vaguely remembered, though, learning in A level History that Mao Tse Tung's strategy included 'withdraw when attacked'. I didn't need telling twice, so we had withdrawn (some might say retreated) back up the hill and waited for people to grow tired of McDonald's. The plan was then to pick our moment to attack and, truly, our retribution would be swift and mighty.

The tactical withdrawal stage, however, was taking longer than I'd envisaged. Things elsewhere had started to settle down fairly soon after the excitement of the great opening. The man with the burger van went back to his old position not far from McDonald's, the kids in the souped-up Vauxhall Novas with the fat tyres and the Wobbly Dobbler stickers had stopped hanging around in the McDonald's car park, frightening the families, and drifted off to more exciting car parks elsewhere. Beatrice's children asked politely if they could come back into the Diner, and were welcomed back like little prodigals. But relatively few

189

customers had drifted back of their own accord, we were losing money, and we were still hiding at the top of the hill like Robert the Bruce in his cave.

Laura stubbed out her fag, and we sat in silence for a while as she gazed out the window, then glanced at the paper, then shifted to the stool. All of a sudden she perked up. 'I know,' she said. 'Why don't I make us both a nice milkshake?'

I opted for a chocolate and caramel shake with a spoonful of broken-up Dime bar mixed in, a hint of mint, cream on the top, and a splatter of white chocolate sauce on the top of that. Every Flavour Milkshakes were one of the little wheezes dreamt up on quiet shifts, to drag customers back from McDonald's, but yet another bright idea had come crashing into the reality of Pareto's Law: people couldn't be bothered to think up 'every flavour', they took ages for the staff to make and, besides, as several of the more sharp-eyed youngsters had pointed out, they weren't really 'every flavour' at all. We didn't do monkey flavour, for a start.

I dozed off again and was woken suddenly by the door opening and a child screaming, 'WANGO DONALS! WANGO DONALS!' It was Dani's baby, now a toddler, with quite a pair of lungs and a fixed idea of what constituted fine dining. Dani looked at me apologetically and shrugged. This was a depressingly common occurrence and I gave her a look that was meant to register that I was familiar with the innately fascist tendencies of toddlers and understood if she wanted to go down the road instead. 'Well, we're not going to McDonald's, we're staying here,' said Dani firmly, much to my surprise, as she dragged the little chap over the threshold.

Laura popped round the counter to give the kid a paper hat and a balloon, and he almost started smiling. Before long he had abandoned his chicken nuggets and was wandering about the place in his new hat, happily playing hide and seek in the kitchen, contrary to one or two health and safety regulations, and swinging on the counter. He and Dani left looking cheerful, but I knew we would have the same battle the next time they came in. Nevertheless, the incident inspired me to start fighting back.

People were complaining that McDonald's was boring. Just what they had imagined was going to happen down there apart from burgers being sold and eaten, I can't imagine, but the general feeling seemed to be that nothing much had changed after all. Despite all the hype, Uckfield still wasn't 'on the map'.

I've always thought that being boring is one of the charms of small town life. I like to imagine that when the first Neolithic youths arrived at 'The Rocks', the surprisingly beautiful lake area just outside town first settled thousands of years ago, they had soon complained that there was nothing to do apart from hunting and gathering, and no doubt exasperated Neolithic parents had yelled at them to stop lolling around the campfire and damn well go and daub something. Anyway, small towns are supposed to be boring, that's why they're small. If they were exciting, more people would go and live in them and they wouldn't be small any more.

Nevertheless, I resolved to rescue Uckfield from the scourge of tedium. Saving the Diner would be but a fringe benefit in the new noble quest to banish boredom from this corner of the Weald. We held a staff meeting (a proper one, with flipcharts and everything), to critically analyse what each of our competitors had that we didn't. First up, McDonald's. The list included easy, safe parking, the play area, extensive seating, lack of waiting time, the drive-thru facility, the low, low prices, the great TV advertising and the Happy Meals.

'Okay,' I told the assembled gathering, as we drifted into Monty Python territory, 'but apart from the easy, safe parking, the play area, the lack of waiting time, the drive-thru, the low, low prices, the great TV advertising and the Happy Meals, what do McDonald's have that we don't?'

'Free toys', said Beatrice.

Maybe we weren't going to beat McDonald's, but what about the other places in town; surely we were a cut above them? We went through the other competitors in turn, the staff hurling insults about them while I struggled to keep up, writing them all down on the flipchart. The general attitude seemed to be that the Little Tea Shoppe was making a fundamental error in opting for a WRVS snack-bar look, and apparently still thought tabards quite the coming thing in which to dress its staff. The Riverside Café seemed not only to be by the Uck, but somehow to have grown out of the Uck; it was decorated in brown and had a damp and muddy feel. The town's speciality cheese emporium (or 'cheesemonger's' as it liked to be known) had recently designated a corner of itself as a coffee shop (or 'coffeemonger's'), but was cold, excessively clean and, frankly, it felt like you were drinking coffee in a cheese shop... and so the list went on.

The conclusion of this strategy session was that Uckfield really was quite boring. There were fifteen takeaway food shops but only one pub in the High Street, and as that was the local for our post-pub crowd it wasn't the obvious choice for a relaxed pint. There were six charity shops (as Harriet Wheeler had pointed out) and three 'Everything £1' shops. We did have a cinema, it's true (God bless Kevin), but you had a long walk to go for a drink afterwards. Life was sapping from the old town, before our eyes, amid a vicious spiral of closing shops, and less and less passing trade. The quality kitchenware shop and the tile shop had gone already; the optician's was serving out its lease; and the owner of the record shop was muttering about 'giving it till Christmas'.

The area was becoming like an elephant's graveyard, with the sad remains of shops being adopted as houses, albeit with large front windows; windows that people still instinctively gazed into expecting to see, say, a nice row of kettles, and being met instead by some poor bloke self-consciously trying to watch the telly.

McDonald's, of course, was at the heart of the new Uckfield – the trading estate, centred on Tesco's, with its convenient parking and one-stop weekly shopping. In this new town centre, once a wide, reedy plain beside the river, car culture had taken over with walkers being actively discouraged from crossing the new retail areas by pointless little barriers, pavements suddenly petering out, and odds and ends of cycle path would start and stop and get you precisely nowhere. A drive-thru McDonald's was simply the apotheosis of that trend.

That week my 'To Do' list read:

1. Reverse the trend towards car domination of Uckfield
2. Save the High Street/make Uckfield fun
3. Start turning a profit

along, of course, with the usual

4. Go running every day!
5. Lose weight
6. Get girlfriend
7. Learn French
8. etc.

I didn't actually have any good ideas about how to reverse car domination, but there were plenty of other things on the list to be getting on with. I moved out of Brighton Marina and nearer to Uckfield, throwing myself into work with an enthusiasm that took even me by surprise. I tried to turn myself into a ruthless machine, single-mindedly blasting all obstacles from my path like a latter-day Napoleon, Rupert Murdoch... Jeffrey Archer. I made endless lists and headed them with Schwarzenegger-esque inspirational messages like 'What doesn't kill you makes you strong' and 'I am a tiger. Rrrrgghh.'

As compensation for the business sliding towards oblivion, we'd never been so well organised, or smart. Yes, yes, it may have been rearranging deckchairs on the *Titanic*, but for the first time we had a standard operating manual detailing how everything should be done, a staff training system with graduated pay structure, cleaning rotas, stock checklists, fridge temperature charts, hazard analysis, an accident book, a marketing budget and a major kick-arse marketing plan.

The best marketing campaign of all, or so Americans will tell you, is to treasure the customers you've already got. They'd say that you should always greet customers by name, send them birthday cards, invite them to be godparent to your first-born, whatever, it doesn't matter as long as you get a sale. But I always found that a bit creepy; I want to keep my customers 'on the team' so to speak, but not start going up a friendship cul de sac, like when people you swapped numbers with on holiday actually call you when you get back to England.

I was also still wrestling with the dilemma of whether to acknowledge to regular customers that they come in all the time or gloss over the subject. Should one, for example, say, 'The usual, sir?' with a light tug on the forelock, or should one show that you take nothing for granted and express surprise and delight at their exquisite taste: 'The beans on toast, Madam, an excellent choice if I may say so?'

As a customer I much prefer the latter approach. At a coffee shop I am known to frequent (nearly every day), the friendly staff say, 'Coffee and a toasted teacake?' and rather pathetically I feel the need to reply, 'Er, no, I'll have the scrambled egg on toast.' I've certainly never forgiven the Indian takeaway that gave me a Christmas card addressed to 'Mr Chicken Dansaak'. I felt it left me looking a little, well, sad. As if the fact that I had the shop on my BT Friends and Family list wasn't bad enough.

Businesses have to appeal to new people, as well, as when you've been in a town for a few years it's easy to get overlooked. I had to remind people that, not only we were still up and running, but we were Uckfield's most exciting offspring – a slightly wild but never boring sort of son, louche and lovable.

Carnival time came round again. I still experienced a faint ripple of embarrassment whenever I thought about my Jeep ride with Elvis, but a crisis is a crisis and this was no time to be faint-hearted. Besides, thousands of people would be out watching and I needed them all to see what a great bunch of guys and girls the Maximum Diner people were. Putting the whole 'reversal of car dominance' project to one side for a moment, I decided to remind people that we did deliveries of big burgers, unlike some other companies I could name, who made manky little burgers that you had to queue up for.

I set to building a giant cheeseburger out of tractor tyres and papier-mâché, six feet wide and four feet high. This would be balanced on top of the Mini I'd bought for deliveries (back when I was flush) and I would drive proudly through the town as part of the procession. Bemused-looking neighbours came out to watch the enormous creation coming together in the garden, under a makeshift marquee to protect it from the rain. My confidence was a little shaken when Mr Lee from the Chinese take-away studied it thoughtfully and then announced that it looked like a giant dogshit. 'Thank you, Mr Lee, and now back to being inscrutable, if you don't mind.' But perhaps he was right? Perhaps I was just wasting my time on yet another rubbish idea. Still, surely it was better than doing nothing?

Remembering that I'd forgotten the vital advertising last time I fixed signs on both sides of the car, saying 'Maximum Diner delivers a BIGGER BURGER'. And then, to prevent the float looking too static (as they do), I coaxed Laura and Sally into marching alongside, wearing matching blue wigs, shiny white miniskirts and thigh-high silver boots (don't ask me why; it was their choice, not mine). They also threw little burger-shaped sweets out to the crowd while prodding the 'burger/dogshit' back on top of the car whenever it began to slide off.

It wasn't terribly subtle, and we failed to secure first place in the Best Float competition, losing to a rather inappropriately jovial display, I thought, from the local funeral director. Once again, however, the following weeks showed no appreciable increase in delivery trade.

Undaunted (okay, a little daunted), phase two of the kick-arse campaign swung into action. The gist of this was that we would concentrate more on our restaurant-ness, and play down the takeaway/delivery elements. I produced a beautiful promotional flyer advertising a series of events and special offers. First up was The Monday Nosebag, where all eat-in food on Monday evenings was half-price. I do think a special offer should be special, and the point of the Monday Nosebag was big piles of food at ludicrously cheap prices; no credit cards, cash only. The idea was that hordes of new people would come in, and on top of the cheap dishes they would add 'cheese-it-all-up' options, get extra chips and spend freely on drinks, which weren't reduced. Then a great roll of positive energy about the Diner would translate into more word-of-mouth recommendations, and higher sales throughout the week.

The downside is that your premises get filled up with cheap-skates and freeloaders. Like the embittered vicar preaching a snotty sermon to people who only turn up at Christmas, I had to get over my annoyance at people who only came to us on Mondays for the cheap food, which was pretty well all of them. Sticking with the religious imagery, I comforted myself with

196

thoughts of Luke 14 verses 15–24, which, for those who may have forgotten, is the parable of the rich man who prepares a banquet but all his friends make excuses for why they can't come. One friend has bought a field, and has to go and see it; another has married a wife, and so cannot come. All familiar excuses! So he commands his servant to go out to 'the streets and lanes of the city and to the highways and the *hedges* [my italics], and bring in the poor and maimed and blind and lame...' Actually that's a pretty good description of the people who did come in on a Monday night.

These half-price sales allowed us to have a busy night where we would otherwise have been banging our heads on the table with boredom and frustration, but the debts were still piling up and I had no prospect of paying them back. I found myself four months behind on payments to suppliers, thousands behind with VAT, cheques were bouncing everywhere. My car would have been repossessed but I hid it. The bank demanded my cards and cheque books back. I felt myself starting to give up.

In all other respects things seemed fine. Beau and I were enjoying long early-morning gallops together over the Downs, and at the Diner we were still all coming up with new marketing ideas and plans for burying McDonald's. But the enthusiasm was going, and a bitterness and cynicism were creeping in. And then Miss Green was knocked down by a car and died in hospital. We heard about it some weeks later and so weren't even able to send flowers. There were no reports in the paper, nothing at all about the death of this remarkable woman. She was just gone.

197

The news would have been upsetting at the best of times, but with my business drifting away I developed a sort of fretful helplessness that did me no good at all when it came to the cut and thrust of debt management.

The psychology of being in financial trouble is interesting. My response to debt (you may have guessed this) was not to open my post or answer my phone, as the financial institutions swarmed around like hyenas attacking a wounded wildebeest. Every £27.50 charged by the bank for a bounced direct debit feels like you're having a chunk bitten out of you, making you weaker and less able to fight back. Eventually you just give up. My mortgage wasn't being paid, and every time the direct debit was returned unpaid I had to pay £25 to the mortgage company as well as the £27.50 to the bank, like a special tax on being poor. Then five days later it would all happen again. A simple payment of a monthly mortgage was costing hundreds of pounds and still not being paid.

Of course, happy, solvent people would simply say that you need to get a grip, talk to the banks and sort the problem out, but that is precisely what people in trouble are unable to do. Instead, the letters pile up and the answerphone is full of messages telling you to call such and such a number and quote such and such a reference number and you erase the messages and slump in front of the television. Though you realise that yelling at call centre staff to 'JUST F***ING WELL F*** OFF YOU F***ERS' when they finally catch up with you isn't the cleverest response, it still feels appropriate, in a dull sort of way, to the situation.

Facing up to a corner of the problem, I visited my doctor and told him that I thought I was getting depressed. I'd rather hoped he'd give me a prescription for Prozac or Valium – I'd always fancied trying those two – but instead he gave me an encouraging chat and a questionnaire to fill in to assess just how unhappy I was. It had multiple-choice questions like in a magazine, only with questions like:

I feel like killing myself... (1) every morning, (2) every evening, (3) all the time, (4) when it rains, (5) I don't, I feel like killing other people.

198

Answering was tricky, because I wanted to seem depressed enough to get the prescription drugs, but not so bad that they sectioned me. A simpler question in my case would have been; 'Has anything happened to seriously screw up your life recently? Say, for example, a giant multinational opening near you and taking away your livelihood?' Though I was impressed at the kindness of the doctor, I really wished he'd just given me some drugs to take the pain of failure away and I'd have taken my chances with chemical dependency later.

The weather wasn't helping, either, as autumn came around wetter than ever. I had to help out on deliveries in order to save paying out for drivers and I was getting wet almost every evening. At the risk of sinking into Dickensian melodrama, both my shoes had holes in them and I ended up with a nasty infection that caused my leg to swell up to twice its normal size. I stomped around the Diner on crutches, bashing things like an old madman and cursing my luck at having to scrape together a business by doing burger deliveries when McDonald's could sit back and wait for customers (my customers), to come to them through their nice, smart, dry drive-thru.

It would have helped if I hadn't been living on my own. The times at work were bearable, but it's when you're left alone that the depression creeps in. That's why farmers get so maudlin – too long stuck on a tractor in a bloody great field. I needed someone to put it all in perspective because although in cosmic, or even global, terms my problems didn't add up to a hill of beans, it doesn't feel like that when your creditors are closing in.

Especially when Mr Sweet, the VAT bailiff, paid another visit. If anything he was a little fatter, which is tactless for a bailiff and made him look even more like a Chaplin-esque villain, but maybe a big build is useful in his profession. Together we went round listing the items he would take away if I didn't find around £4000 within ten days. I tried to direct him toward those

199

items that were not strictly essential for us to trade, albeit in a new minimalist style. The Mini was my first choice because it hardly moved anyway, what with all the rain.

'Don't want it,' he said, his one good eye peering expertly at all my stuff. 'Can't sell that, can I? It's got "Maximum Diner – more haste, more speed" written all over it.' He couldn't take my car either because there was so much finance owing on it that technically I only owned the cigarette lighter and tyres.

'What about the pictures, then? They're worth a bit.'

'No. Don't do art. I'll have the fryer. And the oven, that's worth about fifty quid, and the seats, and the coffee machine, and the crockery, and the fridges.'

'You don't want the fryer,' I said, 'it's got loose wires. It'll kill someone and you'll be responsible. Have the music system instead, and the pot plants, and I'll throw in the kettle.'

An idea was forming to give the Diner a new Japanese theme; no seats, or tables, or music, or plants, or cooking. Instead, rush matting, maybe a kabuki troupe in the corner where the coffee machine was at present, and all the food left raw.

There was no chance of getting that much money together in ten days. The Diner wasn't profitable and I already had thousands more in other debts. To borrow more money from family and friends would be like asking for a massive donation just to keep me in my prison, because it's a miserable life being at the helm of a failing business. Sudden brainwaves come along and you think you have found a way out ('Why, of course, a sushi diner; that's what Uckfield needs!'), before realising that they're foolish notions. ('Idiot! No way are the folk of Uckfield ready for raw blowfish.')

One of the many undermining things about failure is that you always take it personally, and see it as your own fault. My fault for choosing Uckfield, my fault for not beating off McDonald's, my fault for not having a better float at the Carnival, for not getting rid of the yobs who put other people off, for not coming up with better ideas, snazzier menus, hipper design, happier staff, and so on and so on.

The truth is that it's often no one's fault, and the failure probably really will make you a better, wiser, nicer person for the future; but again, it doesn't feel like that at the time. Mr Sweet said he'd be back in ten days, and charged another hundred and fifty quid for the visit. I called the local VAT office and made a futile and humiliating plea for extra time, but was told that effectively I had embezzled the customers' tax money (which, I suppose, is a fair point), and there would be no extra time. I explained that the resale value of the equipment they would take was peanuts compared to what it was worth keeping staff employed, but they'd heard it all before.

The next couple of days were spent in a state of dreamy unreality as I tried to carry on as normal, the impending disaster only bursting into my conscious mind every now and then. It was almost a relief, knowing that soon everything was going to change, but it was upsetting to think that other people would go down, too.

Laura, Liz, Beatrice, Silvio and all the others would be out of a job; the suppliers out of pocket to the tune of thousands of pounds (as if they weren't themselves suffering as a result of their customers losing sales to McDonald's); faithful customers would be coming up to the door all excited at the prospect of a Chicken Barbecue Hash, cheesed up, with a Big Max on the side, an ice-cold Budweiser, maybe a thick slice of cake for pudding, but instead of frisky Laura all they'd find would be a notice on the door from the bailiff. Peering in they might see some papers adrift on the floor, a big pile of post, some chips of wood where

201

they were too rough and broke bits off the furniture as they dragged it out to the van. They'd probably sigh, turn round and trudge back down the hill to McDonald's.

The question was, how to go out gracefully? The fantasy option was to gather up the weekend's takings, leave a note to all concerned, and fly off to an island somewhere. Okay, there wasn't enough cash to fly to an island, but I could afford a coach to Europe. I scanned the map for a place to hide, stuck in a pin in the map, coming up with Slupsk, in Poland. Yes, there lay my destiny, in Slupsk. Maybe I could become a Gentleman of the Road, free to roam and ramble as the fancy took me. That wouldn't be fair to the staff, though. Instead, I decided to tell the staff two days before the bailiffs were due, and to soften the blow we would share out the last week's takings, have a bloody good wake, remove anything we wanted from the premises, cancel the milk, and leave a note on the door for Mr Sweet.

In the meantime I had advertised a Country'n'Western Extravaganza as part of the marketing campaign, and I couldn't get out of it because Laura had bought a pink cowboy hat. I tried to put thoughts of our imminent demise out of my head and set about making it a night to remember. We had advertised an exciting cowboy-style menu, plus tequila, Dolly Parton (not in person), Prettiest Bonnet Competition, Six Shootin' Display (subject to availability), that sort of thing, so I blew the petty cash on all the paraphernalia.

202   The special Western menu included steak, exciting new baked bean recipes, barbecued chicken with corn fritters and special extra hot 'diner-mite' burgers. We put big bowls of guacamole and salsa out, Dolly was playing on CD, Laura looked beautiful in the hat and makeshift tequila holster, and had been practising sliding tequila shots along the bar all week, and we were both prepared to slap our thighs and say 'Yeehah!' – a lot, if necessary.

Pathetic really. It was the kind of nonsense I'd hoped never to get involved in, theme nights being the last desperate resort of the failing restaurant. How often does The Ivy feel the need to put on a 'beach party'? Theme nights are the catering equivalent of sitcoms getting special guest stars in. Customers treated our Country'n'Western Extravaganza with the contempt it deserved and only seven people turned up – four of whom were sheltering from the rain. One was a friend of Adam's who'd come to see Laura in her hat and scrounge some cheap tequila, which left two paying customers, who had turned up for the evening looking puzzled and slightly embarrassed.

To be fair to our Country'n'Western initiative, the rain that evening was of biblical proportions. It thundered down so hard it was flowing down the alleyway and into the back door of the restaurant. Laura and I were suitably dressed in our ten-gallon hats and spent most of the evening either bailing out water, or staring out of the window saying over and over again how we'd never seen so much fucking rain in our entire lives. I'd asked Sally and Liz to come in on their way home from their aikido class in case we were swamped with customers and needed help. As it was we were swamped in leftover tequila, so they gave us a hand in dealing with that. Then we called Sophie and Lucy to help us eat all the steaks, and before long a little party was going. It felt like a leaving party and I toyed with the idea of telling them all there and then that we'd hit the end of the trail, but then I got drunk instead and missed the moment.

Eventually everyone went home, wet, tired and possibly happy, while I fell asleep lying across a couple of seats, fully clothed.

An act of God

I AWOKE TO THE SOUNDS OF A HELICOPTER, circling overhead. It took a while to realise what was going on as I listened to the low thudding sound of the helicopter rotor blades and the pressure of the downdraft, imagining for a while that it was all in my head and that this was perhaps normal for a tequila hangover. Then the helicopter came circling back and, seeing the glow of its powerful searchlight flashing past the window, I decided this might be worth getting up for. Swinging my legs off the banquette that I was uncomfortably squashed into I put my feet in a puddle of water. Oh Jesus, I thought, now we've got a flood.

There couldn't be a flood up here, though, I realised, as my brain clunked into motion; we were right at the top of a hill. Paddling across the floor in the dark I saw with relief that the road outside was clear, the water had come in through the roof and run off from the garden, so it was clear, clean rainwater. As I reheated a mug of last night's coffee in the microwave, and

204

switched on the grill to make a bacon sandwich, I turned on the news to see a GMTV reporter standing on the bypass talking about a river, our river, the Uck, which was a lot closer to him than it should have been.

Grabbing my coat, I raced down the High Street. A river of coffee-coloured water – a hundred yards wide and perhaps five feet deep – was flowing through the town centre. The police were trying to maintain order and keep looters away, which was no easy task as people were trying to escape from houses in the middle of it. The fire brigade had a motor launch out, rescuing the residents of the flats above the shops, and there was a moment of appalled excitement when one of the firemen was swept overboard by the force of the water coming down the alley beside Somerfield; then a cheer as two colleagues efficiently hauled him back in.

I bumped into Beatrice and her children, who excitedly led me through the back alleys to the Tesco's car park. This offered a Grandstand view of McDonald's, with water flowing around and indeed thru it, and one sad, empty car (hopefully the manager's) almost submerged and bobbing around in the water. The helicopter was hovering just behind its golden arches, taking people off roofs and searching for anyone who might be hanging from trees. Then a report came through the grapevine that Vernon Jay, a local jeweller, had been rescued by helicopter after being carried nearly half a mile across town by the torrent of freezing water. A little cheer went up, at last a bit of good news amongst all the misery – except that there wasn't much misery evident. In fact, I'd never seen so many smiling faces in Uckfield. Nobody was pleased at the misfortune befalling so many people but it was just so exciting. For once Uckfield wasn't boring. We'd been on GMTV, for goodness sake! How big time is that?!

It seemed that, as of Thursday October 12th, East Sussex was underwater. Since the start of October it had rained nearly every day, with the usual monthly rain falling in the first ten days. On Tuesday nearly two inches had fallen onto already sodden ground and had filled up the rivers. The heavy Wealden clay and sandstone wouldn't absorb any more water and, as the aquifers filled up, springs that had been dry for centuries suddenly burst forth, much to the surprise of the people whose homes were now built on top of them. On Wednesday and into Thursday night over five inches of rain had fallen. Half that amount would normally be regarded as a once-a-century event.

The river system that the Uck is part of starts just south of Gatwick airport and takes all the water from the west of the county around Haywards Heath, and much of what falls on the Ashdown Forest. All that water was now trying to squeeze itself through one thin valley between the South Downs at Lewes, and it was getting backed up. The run-off alone was so bad that Tesco's was flooded not by the river, but by all the water coming off the playing field behind it.

For now it was just the upriver towns and villages that had flooded, but as high tide approached it was believed that the towns nearer the coast would go under, too. In the circumstances it was amazing that no one had been killed, though Big Vern (as his fellow traders know him) had come closer than most. He had been washed through his shop and out the other side, before being launched across town in a mass of sewage-filled water. He said later that he gave himself up to God, whereupon an island appeared out of nowhere and saved him. He was finally winched to safety by the helicopter from the roof of a semi-submerged business on the industrial estate.

I rang Liz and Laura to ask them to help me open the Diner, but they were busy moving all their furniture upstairs. I said I'd be right over but then suddenly remembered Beau, standing in a meadow by the river near Lewes. Sprinting for the car I drove through flooded roads looking for a good place to try and cross the river. The village of Isfield seemed the best bet, and approaching the river in my four-by-four I thought – Yes! Now is the chance to show that off-roaders aren't just for show.

Repeating the word 'Flood. Flood. Flood. Flood. Flood. Flood. Flood,' over in my head like a mantra, trying to build up courage, I came to the river and saw a great swirling mass of water in front of me. I pictured the car being buffeted by the waves and then flipping over, the water pouring in as I struggled with the seatbelt, being sucked into a whirlpool and dragged to a cold, damp death. Then I repeated the word 'Reverse. Reverse. Reverse. Reverse. Reverse. Reverse,' and drove straight back to Uckfield. The owner of the horse that shared the field with Beau lived on the far side of the river. I phoned her and she promised to move them both to higher ground and look after Beau until the flood subsided.

Liz and Laura had already moved all that could be lifted upstairs so we headed back to the Diner, mopped up, and for the next fourteen hours sold food at a rate never before experienced. Journalists were stacked six to a booth, ordering bacon sandwiches by the armful, while they typed and interviewed and edited photographs for the next day's papers. People with flooded houses and no electricity came in, many didn't even have plates to eat them off as they'd all been doused in sewagey water. Tesco's hadn't opened and Somerfield was still underwater, the roads out of town were impassable, so nobody could go shopping. Nobody could go to work either, many people had no electricity, and everybody else seemed to be too excited to cook.

When we finally closed for the night the water had vanished. I walked down by the river, now back in its canyon but rushing along madly, like it was ready to pop out again at any time. There was an eerie calm about the place, a few police officers hanging

207

around to prevent looting and the first repairmen busily board-
ing up shops, under arc lights, as the electricity was out. There
was flotsam piled up everywhere: sodden books from the town's
two bookshops, cereal packets from Somerfield, videos in their
Blockbuster cases, cartons of Häagen-Dazs ice cream, beds from
Sussex Bed Centre, the entire contents of Superdrug. As I walked
through thick mud in the High Street I slipped on something
that turned out to be the front window of the Riverside Fish Bar.

And that was just in the High Street: according to insurance
companies, 80 percent of the businesses in the industrial estate
were flooded to a depth of three feet or more. While cooking we
had been listening to the local news and it seemed that Lewes
was now underwater, too, with far more disastrous consequences
even than in Uckfield. Beau narrowly avoided the deluge that
rushed into and overwhelmed the floodplains approaching
Lewes, and had been tearing round and round as the cows in the
neighbouring field were drowned, their bodies washing up in
the ruined housing estates a little downriver.

The Diner was constantly packed for the rest of the week, and
then the next and then the next. It was like a reunion of long-lost
customers, and with this crisis we had finally become the centre
of the community. Customers could watch the news together,
sympathise over what they had lost, share experiences, argue
over what had caused it, swap numbers for plumbers and electricians, and get hot food while their own kitchens were covered
in brown sludge.

By the end of the week I was able to pay the VAT, then the suppliers. The flood had saved us.

A few days after the flood, while nipping down to the reopened
Tesco's for emergency supplies, my way was blocked by a bull-

dozer flattening McDonald's. It was a magic moment and I may have emitted a small, guilty whoop.

The other shops at the bottom of town made for a depressing site. Soggy, filthy and abandoned, their windows were streaked with a filthy tidemark from the mud, sewage and oil that had contaminated the water, obscuring the ruined insides and great piles of rotten, sodden merchandise. Since the water had got into the walls and foundations of buildings, plaster would need to be removed, bricks dried out and then replastered, so nothing could reopen until spring. Not that this was a view that impressed the man in the health food shop, who was up and open within days – a much healthier attitude, I think, though that was easy for me to say, sitting pretty at the top of the hill.

I hadn't known that disasters were such big business until the huge pick-up trucks arrived, with Derek's Disaster Relief emblazoned on the side and Red Adair types 'liaising' with the police and fire brigade, strutting about in big macho boots, carrying their tools in huge leather holsters. It looked like the Village People had re-formed and come to sort out Uckfield's problems. And the place looked like it needed them. As well as the flood specialists, the council had chartered fleets of vans to cart off flood-damaged household goods, and everywhere you looked – in the non-flooded as well as flooded areas – people were casting out their old junk, piling the side of the roads with old settees, cookers, carpets and the contents of garages.

Delivering food to flooded homes, I was shown around by customers still stunned by the damage caused by flooding. Many had moved into caravans parked in their driveways as vast industrial heaters blasted away inside their homes; others were treading on precarious walkways where floorboards used to be, having decamped upstairs. I was shocked at how distraught the victims were. For so many of us the whole thing had been an exciting day and a chance to read about Uckfield in the paper, but for the people affected their homes would never feel like their own again. Some tried to be jolly, or to keep a bit of Dunkirk spirit going, but the shock of a pathetic little stream suddenly turning into a chest-high torrent flowing through their living rooms and carrying away their pets and heirlooms was clearly too much to bear.

Still, we could offer a bit of sympathy at the Diner – even to the many old familiar faces who flocked back to us, having been deprived of McDonald's. But that was history and, no matter that it had taken an act of God to return my old customers to the Diner, I was determined to find ways of keeping them. It was time for a rethink, to create a business that could withstand competition, without fear of the bailiffs. And I had that rather smug feeling that time was on my side. The McDonald's site was now a pile of rubble and I could look forward to a few profitable months to replenish company funds before it could hope to trade again.

The bill, please

MY SENSE OF OPTIMISM – of a fresh start for the Diner and a level playing field among us caterers – lasted for just over three weeks. Then, driving home in the middle of the night after another wonderfully busy evening, I was stunned to see four giant lorries slowly trundling along the bypass. Dozens of orange lights were flashing along the side of these massive trucks, along with the flashing blue lights of the police outriders, there to ensure the way was clear through the town. Each lorry had a quarter of a McDonald's restaurant on the back of it and, dismayed as I was, I couldn't help but think that this would make a great float for Carnival night. I was gazing at a brand new style of prefabricated McDonald's that was built to be clipped together easier than an Ikea coffee table.

Driving past in the opposite direction, it felt like a giant 'Game over' sign flashing in front of me. Suddenly it all seemed such a silly little battle. There I was – single, stressed, poor, chasing a dream of bringing quality burgers, cooked to order and with a range of tasty toppings, to the good people of Uckfield... and it all seemed a bit, well, trivial. As a child, being driven for the first time through the outskirts of London, I remember being struck by the dingy little shops with filthy windows and stuff inside that no one could possibly want. I'd thought how tragic and point-less it would be to have that as your life's work. And that night I sensed that I wasn't in a much better position myself. My life had come down to an unwinnable battle to sell more slices of minced and griddled cow than the guy (or, more accurately, the multi-national corporation outlet) down the road.

Maybe if I felt I had any chance of winning, my disillusion would have been less than total, but we all knew that the Uckfield crowd would be back to McDonald's before you could say 'Happy Meal'.

Enough was enough; it was time to jump shop.

McDonald's was duly clipped together and within three weeks of the flood, adding insult to injury, the Mayor officially reopened it again, and the cubs turned out, again. Then there was another flood. Oh, if only. The stormy weather continued and the river bubbled up again and the word on the streets was that if McDonald's flooded again they were pulling out for good. I tried to persuade Silvio to run into McDonald's on a busy Saturday lunchtime dressed as a fireman and yell, 'GET OUT, GET OUT! SHE'S GOING TO FLOOD! GET OUT NOW! LEAVE YOUR BURGERS AND FLEE, FLEE, FLEE TO THE HILLS!' but he just looked at me sadly. Then I toyed with the idea of pushing the Mini into the Uck, hoping to disrupt the flow just enough. I'm sure, had he been in my position, the young Ray Kroc would have tried it. But I didn't.

As the waters receded and the ground started drying out, I put the business up for sale – feeling very much like Judas must have done before he got his hands on the forty pieces of silver. When I was buying commercial property I had thought it dishonest and silly that owners wanted to keep the sale secret from the staff, not least because it meant viewing shops at ridiculous hours of the morning or during the night. I knew of one Uckfield café where the manager swore blindly to his staff that he wasn't selling up, even with the premises on display in an estate agent's window two hundred yards away. Yet, when it came to my own business I also kept it quiet, telling myself that I shouldn't spoil the happy atmosphere until I knew for sure what was happening.

Being new to the game I paid two agents to sneak in during one of my solo shifts and value the property. The first was an affable, clubby sort of chap who sat drinking coffee and discussing his own restaurant for an hour, had a quick shimmy round, trousered a non-refundable valuation fee of £300 and said I might get £60,000 but I should ask for £65,000; £55,000 would see it sold in a week if I was desperate. The other one, Sue, was the kind of woman I try to avoid. She was brusque and businesslike and treated me with the sort of withering contempt that I once got from Amanda's more mercenary friends. Sue charged £400 but did at least go through the books and establish a valuation based on more than three cups of coffee and an informal natter. When she'd gone I saw that I'd signed her up as sole agent, meaning that she got her commission even if I sold it through the first agent and even, within a specified period, if I sacked her. So, she was tricky; I like that in an agent. She thought £40,000 would be an optimistic value to aim for and got stroppy when I insisted on £65,000.

Signing the agency documents left me feeling both guilty and free, giving me an idea of what divorce might be like. Sitting at

213

the table with the forms, I remembered all the plans I'd made and discussions we'd had about the future. I couldn't bear to look at the place, so I just kept my head down and signed the papers.

Two months later I dropped the price to £45,000, as the impact of the new, even brighter, shinier McDonald's started hitting home. Like Kevin before me, though, I would have taken much less and, despite resolving to make our remaining time together really special, once the big decision had been taken I really just wanted to get away.

Eventually I got a phone call from someone called Ali, who said he was interested in buying. He agreed to come at midnight, after his shift at a kebab shop ended, so I quickly drove the staff home and then returned to the Diner to have a tidy-up (but then worried that he might think we weren't busy if it was too spick and span and so messed it all up again). Twenty minutes later I had sold the place for £43,000.

It was an intense twenty minutes, and the most exciting business experience I'd had at the Diner, as we locked horns in a titanic verbal battle. Erroneous arguments were batted away contemptuously and awkward points glossed over with more assurance than I felt.

Ali had brought with him his older brother Touran, who wandered around while we spoke, shouting the odd Turkish phrase back at Ali. It wasn't a language I understand, but the tone seemed outraged.

'Your brother seems impressed,' I commented breezily.

'He says the equipment is shit,' said Ali.

'Precisely! So if I can take so much money with this stinking load of old garbage, just think how much you'll make with all your new stuff!' I reasoned coolly.

And so we went on.

Ali and his brother were Kurdish Turks, who lived in nearby Heathfield. Ali had been trying to open his own café or kebab shop for years but had come up against a planning brick wall. At the time I thought him a fool for not offering me £20,000 and pleading (lying) that it was all he had, then leaving it another month before offering me £25,000, which I would have taken gratefully. Then again, seeing how much he was planning to invest on improvements to the Diner, I cursed myself for not sticking with the original price. He obviously loved the place and, while Touran (whose spoken English was restricted at the time to grunts and odd facial tics) was kicking the equipment and snorting contemptuously, he was staring rapturously at the dining area.

Maybe they were working a good Kurd, bad Kurd routine on me, for before I knew it I'd come down two grand and was shaking their hands and thinking, Bollocks – that would have paid for a round-the-world air ticket.

The next day I confessed to the staff. They'd been puzzled for some time at my easygoing attitude: stroppy customers were given full refunds and only the most lacklustre of sarcasm, while delivery drivers ringing in sick were told to stay in bed and jolly well look after themselves. It wasn't like me at all.

As news of the sale spread, a knee-jerk racism seemed to take hold, one that took me by surprise, considering how many foreign members of staff we'd employed over the years. Suppliers, window cleaners, even customers, seemed to think themselves at liberty to make insulting comments about 'the Turks'. I tried to point out that Ali was a businessman who not only wanted to keep all the staff but planned to sink good money into making the Diner work. Then I caught myself explaining that, as a Kurd, he probably didn't even consider himself Turkish at all, realised I had sunk to their level and gave up trying. As the time for the handover came nearer I wielded what little authority I had left to insist that Ali be treated politely when he arrived.

The solicitors dragged on interminably and in the meantime Ali came to work at the Diner to learn the cooking and soothe a few of the doubters. He soothed them rather too well for my liking, as before long the staff were milling around and chatting about various improvements they'd like to see, and were even volunteering to stay later on his busier shifts. Ali undeniably had charm and might be thought quite handsome, in a rather obvious tall and dark sort of way, but it's a bit much when you're made to feel redundant in your own Diner. The last straw was when I came in one afternoon to find Liz and the bakery delivery man flicking through some Turkish holiday brochures with Ali and chatting about the Turquoise Coast. I suggested Ali spent his last week of freedom at home with his family while I enjoyed my diner in peace.

On my last night we had a party for favourite customers, who got free food and champagne. This was followed by a leaving party during which a game of truth or dare got out of hand, as they're wont to do, with Liz repeatedly asking me if I fancied Emma, our new part-time delivery driver. In truth I fancied her rotten, ever since she'd phoned back for directions from a housing estate and launched into a comic sketch about the exaggeratedly rural street names – Woodpecker Way, Barn Close, Fetlock Avenue, Set-Aside Street, and the like. But like all good Englishmen I kept silent under interrogation, far too silent in fact. By the end of the game, an equally embarrassed Emma had her coat on and was arranging a lift back with Silvio. Then, as if to spell out vividly what I might have just blown, two drunken regulars started making passionate love on one of the tables.

216

There was nothing either of us could do other than rescue the condiments and wait on the street for a chance to finish locking up. (The table was number two, under the low roof, by the way, in case anyone wants to avoid it.)

The next morning found me standing alone in the Diner, stranded between outrageous feelings of sentimentality and a revulsion at the idea of cooking any more burgers. I went round touching everything: the tiles I'd grouted, the mural I painted, the pictures I'd picked out, the utensils I'd cooked so many thousands of Big Maxs with. The call came in that the money had been received; I cooked a last barbecue hash and coleslaw for myself, locked up and walked away.

Then halfway down the High Street I stopped, ran back, unlocked the door and grabbed a couple of pictures off the wall. Then I took my favourite knife, and the best CDs, and some glasses and plates as souvenirs, and the US Army helmet, a teaspoon, a mug, and some T-shirts, and a couple of menus, and... Eventually I had such a big pile of souvenirs I had to bring the car round to load it up. I left a pile of cash to cover it all, then slunk off quickly before Ali could arrive to see the great gaps on the wall where the pictures had been.

Epilogue

IN THE IMMEDIATE AFTERMATH of selling the Diner I didn't quite know what to do with myself. I was out of jail and my troubles were over. I could go out of an evening, I had money. I could do anything. Faced with so many possibilities, I sat mulling them over *chez moi*, ordering takeaway food and catching up on eight years of missed *Neighbours* from the safety of my settee. Oh, lists were written. Exciting internet sites with 'escape' in the title were surfed. But at 10 o'clock each morning I was still looking at my watch and wondering if Liz had remembered to wake up and go to work, or thinking I should check the chip delivery.

This lasted for about three weeks, and then I experienced a minor epiphany similar to realising that you've finally, definitely given up smoking, and I thought: Bloody hell – I got away with it! Which sent me too far the other way, swanning around like a cross between a newly-freed mafia don, and a paroled Jonathan Aitken, ringing up his old mates and inviting them round for

Bible study. But slowly I began to realise that nobody else saw my reappearance as the end of a great odyssey, or, at least, if they did, they weren't bothered. From there on it was plain sailing.

And so it has worked out. It's nearly two years on now, and I'm waiting outside the Anchor (yes, the pub with the plastic canoes) for Emma to join me. The sun that's been beating down all day has dropped low and a welcome breeze filters through the trees beside the Ouse. Somewhere up in one of them is my Frisbee. Bess, useless mother of Biggie, has been given to me as a present by my sister since I've 'got so much spare time these days', and now she's rampaging around the pub garden, giving the swans the Gary B treatment and distracting me from the business of scribbling notes.

For I've been pursuing a rather different path to the hard, grimy, stressful work of catering. I enrolled on a journalism course and then, egged on by my screenwriting brother, began writing a book to plug that gap in the market, for books about small town restaurants. Writing is a career choice almost as financially precarious as running a Diner, but I've been getting by – and mirroring Emma's unsociable hours – by taxi driving in Newhaven and the East Sussex area.

Life is good. There's a lot more cachet in profiling TV celebs than in serving them burgers, and I like the simple work of night-time cabbing that gives you plenty of time to let your imagination wander. Lately, though, while driving around Newhaven, my mind has been drifting back to the world of restaurants, and not just to write this book. The Diner idea has been calling me back, and as I drive around Newhaven at night I can't help checking out empty premises. This is a town in dire need of some catering know-how. There's not much here other than a McDonald's (inevitably – but we know about them) and a Brewster's, which is a 'family-pub-restaurant'. You know Brewster's is a family-pub-restaurant because, on the hour, every hour, one of the waitresses disappears into a back room, puts on a furry costume, and emerges as Brewster Bear to play with the children. You don't get that in the Red Lion.

Perhaps I'll suggest dressing up as a bear to Ali next time I'm in Uckfield. Not that I do go back there very often, though Ali is always welcoming, and even Touran will offer me a cappuccino when I wander in. Frankly, I can't understand why they're making money now when I never did. Despite McDonald's, despite new competition from Pizza Express and Simply Italian! and a big new café-bar just down the road, the Diner is not only surviving but thriving. My own theory is that Uckfield has reached a kind of tipping point, and people are now coming out to the town because it has such a number of restaurants.

Is it too arrogant to believe that the Maximum Diner might have started that? Well, yes, it is. But from a distance, and since starting writing about my Diner career, I'm beginning to see where I went wrong – economically speaking, at least.

So I'm thinking that maybe if I had another go I could get it right. With bigger premises, neither at the top of a hill nor in the valley, but halfway up. Then I could make the franchise idea work. And, if this book sells enough copies, that's what I'm going to do. I'm going to open a new Maximum Diner and make it even bigger in Newhaven.